S. HRG. 113–299

S. 919, THE DEPARTMENT OF INTERIOR TRIBAL SELF–GOVERNANCE ACT OF 2013

HEARING

BEFORE THE

COMMITTEE ON INDIAN AFFAIRS
UNITED STATES SENATE

ONE HUNDRED THIRTEENTH CONGRESS

SECOND SESSION

JANUARY 29, 2014

Printed for the use of the Committee on Indian Affairs

U.S. GOVERNMENT PRINTING OFFICE
WASHINGTON : 2014
88–302 PDF

CONTENTS

S. 919, THE DEPARTMENT OF INTERIOR TRIBAL SELF–GOVERNANCE ACT OF 2013

WEDNESDAY, JANUARY 29, 2014

U.S. SENATE,
COMMITTEE ON INDIAN AFFAIRS,
Washington, DC.

The Committee met, pursuant to notice, at 2:30 p.m. in room 628, Dirksen Senate Office Building, Hon. Maria Cantwell, Chairwoman of the Committee, presiding.

OPENING STATEMENT OF HON. MARIA CANTWELL, U.S. SENATOR FROM WASHINGTON

The CHAIRWOMAN. The Senate Indian Affairs Committee will come to order.

Today we are doing two things. One, having a business session on two legislative matters, the re-vote on Vince G. Logan to be Special Trustee, Office of the Special Trustee, and S. 1448 to provide for equitable compensation to the Spokane Tribe of Indians of the Spokane Reservation for the use of tribal land. That is legislation that we have had before in this Committee and passed out of this Committee and passed out of the Senate and the House, just never passed at the same time. So we wanted to also give that an opportunity to be moved.

So while we are waiting for members to come, I will go ahead and give my opening statement as it relates to both of those issues. And then we will see where we are as far as a quorum.

Today, as I said, the Committee is here to consider two legislative items and then have a legislative hearing on tribal self-governance. We have a real good set of witnesses so I look forward to hearing their comments as well.

But the Committee previously heard from Mr. Logan and the Committee reported his nomination to the full Senate before the session ended. Mr. Logan's nomination has since been resubmitted for this session of Congress and it requires our Committee to act again. Hopefully we can act judiciously today and enact that.

The Special Trustee is charged with overseeing the Department of the Interior's fulfillment of its trust responsibilities to tribes and individual Indians. The Special Trustee also implements any necessary trust reforms at the Department of Interior and ensures that they are consistent with the government's trust responsibility. Mr. Logan has shown a great deal of passion for working with tribes and individual Indians to manage their trust assets. The Committee appreciates his willingness to take on this difficult role.

The second item, as I mentioned, was S. 1448, the Spokane Tribe of Indians of the Spokane Reservation Equitable Compensation Act. A version of this bill has been considered previously by this Committee and some more versions have passed out of the Senate and the House. So I am hopeful that in this Congress this issue can finally be put to rest.

I originally introduced a version of this bill along with my colleague from Washington, Senator Murray, on September 10, 2013, and the Committee held a legislative hearing receiving testimony from both the Spokane Tribe and the Administration supporting this bill. The bill would compensate the Spokane Tribe for past and future use of land by the United States for operation of the Grand Coulee Dam. And today the tribe has only received $4,700 since the government flooded 1,000 acres of Spokane tribal lands to construct and operate this dam. This bill will finally provide the tribe with the equitable compensation for their use of land.

I will be offering an amendment in the nature of a substitute today that addresses how the annual payments to the tribes will have no effect on current ratepayers. But before we get to that, I might ask my colleague, the Vice Chairman of the Committee, if he has any opening statements or comments that he would like to make.

STATEMENT OF HON. JOHN BARRASSO, U.S. SENATOR FROM WYOMING

Senator BARRASSO. Just briefly. Thank you. Today we are going to be considering your bill, the Spokane Equitable Compensation Act, I know this is very important to you and to the Spokane Tribe. So I appreciate you and your staff continuing to work diligently to address the issues of the bill, especially the cost. Thank you for that.

We are also going to consider the nomination of Mr. Logan as Special Trustee. This position is important to the Federal Government in carrying out its trust responsibility and Mr. Logan's strong financial background, I believe, is going to serve him well. If confirmed as Special Trustee, his experience will be needed to help improve the Indian Trust Administration. So again, I thank you for your leadership on both these important matters.

The CHAIRWOMAN. Great. Thank you for that. I don't know if any of my colleagues have anything else they want to comment on, questions for staff?

Senator BARRASSO. If I could, Madam Chair, just before I relinquish my time, this business meeting and this hearing may be the final one with you as Chair of this Committee, I understand. So before I yield, I just want to state that it really has been a privilege for me to serve with you on this Committee and in this capacity. So I am hoping you remain with us at least on the Committee. I am honored that I could serve with the first woman to chair this Committee. You have set an incredible standard for the Committee by providing clear, competent and collegial leadership.

I also want to compliment your entire staff for working closely with mine on matters before the Committee. So thank you for the cooperation. It has come wonderfully. If your time happens to be cut short as chair for good reason, I wish you the very best in your new endeavors, whatever they may be, and extend a heartfelt thanks to you for your diligent work in improving the lives of Indian people. Thank you, Madam Chair.

The CHAIRWOMAN. Thank you. I want to thank the Vice Chair for his leadership. I may be, what, the third member you have worked with as ranking member? So I guess that says that we are leaving a great deal up to you for continuity with the Committee. And thank you for your comments.

I do believe this may well be my last hearing to chair as Chair of this Committee. And I have to say it is with great regret that I leave this position. Because it has only been a short tenure here. And I have a great deal of passion for Indian Country and the issues that affect them.

So I am definitely not leaving the Committee and I am not leaving that passion. I am just turning the reins over to a very qualified member of our Committee, Senator Tester, who I am very excited, after being in Montana this summer, he and I, visiting a lot of Indian Country, I am very excited to have him take on this new role and responsibility. I am just going to double my efforts in working with all of you on these important issues, because there is still a lot to do.

I certainly want to thank my staff, because they have worked hard on a variety of issues this year and have put forth a variety of ideas. We appreciate that. Indian Country has continually changed and improved in providing for new economic opportunities for themselves and the communities around them. That is what we are excited about and we want to keep working to preserve those economic opportunities moving forward. So I know there is a lot to do on that.

Senator Tester?

STATEMENT OF HON. JON TESTER,
U.S. SENATOR FROM MONTANA

Senator TESTER. I just want to echo the ranking member's appreciation for your leadership and your vision for this Committee. I too hope that you stay on this Committee and remain a valuable contributor to the conversation. Because I think you have been great in the position of Chairman and the poor soul that has to follow you has to live up to those expectations.

So we thank you for your leadership and your vision.

The CHAIRWOMAN. Thank you. I appreciate that very much.

As I said, my heart is definitely heavy here, because I have a great deal of passion for these issues and representing 29 different organizations from our region, these are very, very important issues. We just have to keep pushing ahead.

I think we are one member short of the quorum that we need to move out these two nominations and hopefully someone is on their way to do that, on either side of the aisle. If I could, I think I am just going to go ahead and read my opening statement while they are here on the legislative hearing to follow, which is, many of my colleagues know that the importance of tribal self-governance has been a big issue for this Committee. We are going to be hearing about the Tribal Self-Governance Act of 2013.

4

S. 919, I think everybody understands the importance of the Self-Determination Act of 1975, because the Act provided a shift in the way the Federal Government provides services in Indian Country, providing tribes with the authority to take over those services and tailor them to meet their communities. The self-governance provisions that have been added over the past 25 years have provided tribes with greater flexibility and control of how Federal funds are used in their communities and tribal control of these programs provided greater job opportunities and better services for tribal members.

We have not always had great success in improving conditions in Indian Country over the years, but I think it is safe to say that the policies of self-determination and self-governance have been the most successful policies in U.S. history in dealing with tribal governments. I am sure we are going to hear more about that today.

Self-governance began with only seven tribes in 1991, now over half of all federally-recognized tribes have self-governance agreements with the Department of the Interior for Indian Health Services. These 300 tribes are utilizing over $400 million in Federal funding to provide services to their communities. While the programs have been successful, there are always improvements that can be made.

So S. 919 is the culmination of discussions between tribal leaders and the Department of the Interior and other stakeholders that would streamline the self-governance process. Currently tribes must use different negotiation processes for the Department of the Interior and Indian Health Services. S. 919 would make that a similar process.

This bill has many other common sense provisions relating to the negotiation process, such as negotiating in good faith, timelines on decision-making, providing specific reasons that the Secretary of the Interior can decline the self-governance compact or funding agreement. The Department of the Interior testified in support of similar legislation in the House in the last Congress, so I am eager to hear their thoughts on this bill and how it continued to evolve and hear concerns by both the tribes and the Administration.

I also want to thank our tribal witnesses for testifying today. They represent tribes and tribal consortiums that have been participating in self-governance for 20 years. So certainly they have been the pioneers in this particular area. I know that they can continue to suggest how we improve the self-governance program as well.

I particularly want to thank Chairman Ron Allen of the Jamestown S'Klallam Tribe, a real leader in the self-governance movement. And I appreciate his traveling all this way to be here for these discussions as well.

We will look forward to hearing from all of these members, including the Honorable Ron Trahan from the Confederated Salish and Kootenai Tribes in Montana and Jerry Isaac, President of the Tanana Chiefs Conference, a consortium of Alaska Native villages. And finally, we will hear form Mickey Peercy, the Executive Director of self-governance for the Chocktaw Nation of Oklahoma.

So again, I just want to say in advance of that part of our hearing today that we will get to you in just a second.

[Whereupon, the Committee proceeded to other business:]

The CHAIRWOMAN. So now we are going to back to the hearing. And I don't know if any of my other colleagues want to make an opening statement. I mentioned the individuals that we are going to be hearing from. In the first panel, we are going to hear from Kevin Washburn. So if Kevin can come up to the table for his part, and then I mentioned the names of those who will be on the second panel. Do any of my other colleagues want to make a statement? Yes, Senator Murkowski.

STATEMENT OF HON. LISA MURKOWSKI, U.S. SENATOR FROM ALASKA

Senator MURKOWSKI. Thank you, Madam Chairman. I will be brief here. I want to thank you for scheduling the hearing along with the Vice Chairman here.

Indian self-determination has been in my mind the most successful Federal Indian policy, given the difficult history that our Nation's indigenous people have had with the policies here in the United States. When our tribes can manage their own programs, I think they are better equipped to address the disparities that exist within our Native populations.

I am pleased to be a co-sponsor of the bill. In Alaska, we continue to experience the failed management of our lands from thousands of miles away by Federal agencies here in D.C. Many of our Native communities live right next to and within the boundaries of our public lands, our national parks and our wildlife refuges.

I have stated as the ranking member on the Energy and Natural Resources Committee that I would like to see self-governance agreements supported and expanded by the Administration. In Alaska, the Department of Interior has the authority to use self-governance agreements to contract out many operations, functions with tribes at nearly all of the public land units in the State. And yet we only have two of these in existence.

So I have called on the National Park Service and U.S. Fish and Wildlife, to recommit themselves to advocating and advancing these agreements which not only help Alaska Natives connect with their land but be part of subsistence management. I understand that this bill preserves the authority of the Secretary of the Interior to authorize the inclusion of non-BIA programs and contracts and funding the agreements, local management really means that our tribes can continue to practice their customary and traditional hunting and fishing.

I would also like to make a special note and welcome President Jerry Isaac of the Tanana Chiefs Conference. He has termed out as president of TCC in March. Jerry, I would just like to publicly thank you for your dedication, for your commitment, for your leadership for the Tanana Chiefs region. I have always valued your guidance and wisdom and know that you will continue in that.

So we are pleased to have him here before the Committee today. Thank you, Madam Chair.

The CHAIRWOMAN. Vice Chairman Barrasso?

Senator BARRASSO. Thank you, Madam Chairwoman. I just want to thank you for holding this hearing. The 1975 Act enacted by Congress, the Indian Self-Determination and Education Assistance

Act, designed to advance a more effective dynamic for Federal tribal relations. Since then, there have been improvements in both the Federal tribal relationship and the delivery of service. I think it is important that today we consider S. 919, which I have co-sponsored with you.

This bill is intended to build upon those improvements, enhance the delivery of services. It is the product of many years of work by the tribes, by the Administration, by Congress. I look forward to hearing how this bill addresses the interests of stakeholders and improves services.

Thank you, Madam Chairwoman.

The CHAIRWOMAN. Thank you.

I want to add an addendum to my previous comments. It certainly has been an honor working with you as the Vice Chairman of this Committee. And it has been a smooth working process. I appreciate your staff and the collaboration between our offices. So I can definitely say that Indian Country has had a good partner in working through your office. So we certainly appreciate working with you in the future on this Committee.

So thank you. We decided that we both had a love for "yes." And I don't mean just voting aye, but a love for an organization that someday will make it into the rock and roll hall of fame called yes.

But anyway, we will now turn to the Honorable Kevin Washburn to hear his testimony from the Department of Interior. Thank you for being here today as the Assistant Secretary for Indian Affairs. If you could just give us your thoughts on where we need to go on self-governance.

STATEMENT OF HON. KEVIN WASHBURN, ASSISTANT SECRETARY—INDIAN AFFAIRS, U.S. DEPARTMENT OF THE INTERIOR

Mr. WASHBURN. Thank you, Madam Chair, Vice Chairman and members of the Committee. It is an honor to be here, as usual, thank you.

Let me echo the thanks, Madam Chair, for your service. It is really appropriate that you actually chaired this hearing, because the original Self-Determination bill in 1975 was sponsored by Scoop Jackson. And Mark Trahant has written a terrific little book about the passage of that. So it is nice to have someone from the State of Washington, a Senator from the State of Washington presiding over this.

The CHAIRWOMAN. If I could just interject, we certainly lament the passing of Forrest Gerard, who is featured in that book as one of the pioneers of Indian policy here in Washington, D.C., and was a great hero. That book talks about all that he did to move Indian policy in a new direction. He just recently passed, so I wanted everybody to know how appreciative we were of his service to our Country.

Mr. WASHBURN. Thank you, Chairwoman. That underscores the importance of all the staff around the room, because that is often who helps get all of this done. So thank you. And his passing was tough. He was the first person to have held my job, actually, during the Carter Administration, when this position was elevated to an assistant secretary position.

He died over the holidays, and I was able to go out to the funeral. It was a sad day, but he was well celebrated and he accomplished a lot, not the least of which was turning this whole ship of state toward self-determination, which has been, as several of you said, the most successful policy toward American Indian tribes this Nation has ever had. It was started in 1975 with the Indian Self-Determination Education Assistance Act, which was updated in 1998, when the self-governance demonstration project was created to allow compacts with tribes that were broader than just contracts. That was made permanent in 1994.

As you said, Madam Chair, in your opening statement, we have a lot of tribes that are now engaged in the self-governance effort. And frankly, we are doing a lot better job meeting the trust responsibility when it is Indian tribes that are providing those services directly to their people, rather than through Federal officials.

And I think that is largely because of accountability. Tribal leaders are just much more accountable to their populations and they know better the needs of their population than general schedule Federal employees ever could, even though everybody at the BIA and the BIE and IHS and other agencies who often have tribes' best interests at heart, they can't ever know the tribes' best interests as well as their own elected officials do.

So I believe that that accountability has made this a very good regime. I believe it is now time to improve the regime even more and I think that is what S. 919 does. So I ask you all for your support of S. 919.

I don't need to go a whole lot deeper than that. I have written testimony and I have read the very good testimony by each of the other witnesses, some of whom have been at the forefront of self-determination and self-governance for a very, very long time. I am grateful for their work.

Aside from accountability, I think the other thing that self-governance brings to tribes is flexibility. Tribes need flexibility in how to provide services, and the self-governance compacts provide that. And S. 919 will enhance that flexibility even more.

I have a couple of members of my staff here who work really hard on these issues, Hank Ortiz and Sharee Freeman. They are the ones who work where the rubber meets the road on these issues. And we are supportive of S. 919. We are working on some little tweaks to the language to address concerns by the IHS and Bureau of Reclamation. But we are supportive of the legislation overall and certainly the intention of the legislation.

[The prepared statement of Mr. Washburn follows:]

PREPARED STATEMENT OF HON. KEVIN WASHBURN, ASSISTANT SECRETARY—INDIAN AFFAIRS, U.S. DEPARTMENT OF THE INTERIOR

Good afternoon, Chairwoman Cantwell, Vice Chair Barrasso, and members of the Committee. My name is Kevin Washburn. I am the Assistant Secretary for Indian Affairs at the Department of the Interior (Department). Thank you for the opportunity to provide testimony on behalf of the Department on S. 919, the Department of the Interior Tribal Self-Governance Act of 2013.

S. 919 seeks to amend both Title I and Title IV of the Indian Self-Determination and Education Assistance Act (ISDEAA) (25 U.S.C. § § 450 *et seq.*). In more than 200 years of federal Indian policy, the policies of self-determination and self-governance that have developed during the past four decades have produced, by far, the most successful relationship between the United States and its tribes. These policies have also increased tribal governmental capacities and improved services to Indian people.

The Administration strongly supports the principles of self-determination and self-governance, and consistent with this support we believe the ISDEAA should be strengthened to make it work better for the Federal Government and for Indian tribal governments. Accordingly, the Administration supports S. 919.

President Obama recognizes that federally recognized Indian tribes are sovereign, self-governing political entities that have a government-to-government relationship with the United States, as expressly recognized in the United States Constitution. Secretary Jewell, too, is a strong supporter of the principle of tribal self-determination, the principles of the ISDEAA, and is committed to working to further tribal self-governance.

In 1975, the Congress enacted the ISDEAA, Pub. L. No. 93–638. Title I allows a tribe to contract individual programs away from the Department and operate the programs as, in essence, tribal programs. Title I also gives a tribe the latitude to redesign and rebudget Federal programs that it assumes.

In 1988, Congress enacted Title III of the ISDEAA as a demonstration project, which allowed an Indian tribe to contract several programs from the Department, and allowed Indian tribes to reallocate funds and redesign those programs to best benefit their communities. In 1994, Congress made the demonstration project permanent in Title IV of the ISDEAA, Pub. L. No. 103–413.

Title IV provides resources to Indian tribes, enabling them to plan, conduct, consolidate, and administer programs, services, functions, and activities for tribal citizens according to priorities established by their tribal governments. Under Title I and Title IV, Indian tribes have greater control and flexibility in the use of these funds, reduced reporting requirements, and the authority to redesign or consolidate programs, services, functions, and activities. Title I and Title IV generally allow Indian tribes to reallocate funds during the year and carry over unexpended funds into the next fiscal year without Secretarial approval. As a result, these funds can be used with more flexibility to address each Indian tribe's unique condition.

Funding agreements under the ISDEAA have helped to strengthen government-to-government relationships with Indian tribes. Self-determination and self-governance tribes have been good managers of the programs they have undertaken. Many times, tribal governments add their own resources to the programs and are able to fashion programs to meet their needs and the particular needs of their members. Tribal governments are often better suited than the Federal Government to address the changing needs of their members. Indian tribal governments have often observed that, when they are working under self-determination contracts and self-governance funding agreements, they are not viewed by the Federal Government as just another Federal contractor, but rather that their work reflects a true government-to-government relationship characterized by mutually agreed-to responsibilities and tribal empowerment.

For nearly a decade, Indian tribes have asked Congress to update Title I and Title IV to address various issues, to include more non-BIA programs, and to streamline the process of negotiating annual funding agreements. S. 919 goes a long way toward accomplishing these goals. Non-BIA programs, however, often have different characteristics that suggest a more tailored approach to the specific programs. For example, the Bureau of Reclamation uses a methodology in its budget formulation that is different from BIA's methodology because of the nature of Reclamation's appropriations for large projects. Section 202 of S. 919 is intended to address those differences, and the Department looks forward to working with the Committee to ensure section 202 meets that objective.

The Department recognizes the need for the self-determination and self-governance programs to evolve to improve and increase the frequency of funding agreements. The Administration is proud to report that, after a series of negotiations with tribal stakeholders that began over three years ago, we reached agreement on a number of issues and the language is embodied in S. 919. Our agreement on this critical legislative priority for Indian County reflects the Administration's commitment to restore the integrity of the government-to-government relationship with Tribal Nations. The Native American communities in this country confront many challenges, and this Administration is committed to working with Tribal Nations to create opportunities for all of our communities to thrive and flourish.

This concludes my prepared statement. I will be happy to answer any questions the Committee may have.

The CHAIRWOMAN. Thank you for that testimony. I do have a question for you about various tribes and why it has worked in some areas and why others have been more reluctant. But I have to ask you about this contract support question, because we had a little bit of success in the fiscal year 2014 budget. I want to thank my colleague, Senator Murkowski, because she has been a loud voice in making sure that our budget reflected not having a cap.

So my question is, does the Department have a plan on how it is going to pay contract support costs moving forward since there is no longer a cap in place?

Mr. WASHBURN. Yes, Madam Chair, we are working on a plan. One of the things we need to do, so the process for us now is to develop an operating plan that we submit to OMB and then back to the Appropriations Committee to explain how we are going to operate for the rest of the year on the Omnibus Bill. We are wrestling with that, and we are consulting with tribes about that. We have a call on Monday, both IHS and the Indian Affairs at Interior have a call with tribal leaders on Monday, set up by the White House, to consult about that.

The Administration had rolled out a plan to cap that those contract support costs, which was done without any consultation with tribes and was soundly rejected by tribes and by Congress.

The CHAIRWOMAN. And the courts.

Mr. WASHBURN. Well, sure, and the courts, too in some respects.

So we are trying to figure out how to go forward. Honestly, the Appropriations bill punted the issue back to us. They basically said, we are not going to adopt caps, and we are remanding the issue back to you to figure out how to meet contract support costs.

I personally know how important contract support costs are to the ability of tribes to do these jobs that we ask them to do. And I think that we would like to get to a place where we can provide full contract support cost funding. We think we are headed in that direction. But we need to consult with tribes about how that will work, and we are anxious to start that and then to submit our operating plan and get approval.

The CHAIRWOMAN. The reason I am bringing this up now, I certainly want to emphasize the success that we have had, thanks again to everybody on this Committee and I think a previous hearing trying to escalate the issue with those in the Administration to understand the court decision and where we have been. Certainly taking off the cap allows for a solution to be had. I don't think it is just kicking the problem back, saying let's consult. It's basically us saying, let's make sure that there is fair compensation.

The reason I am bringing this up is because I have detected some tribes in their discussions and thoughts about self-governance thinking, well, I like the formula that I have now. People are concerned, if they move toward self-governance, are they going to get the aid and support, or are you going to have another contract support issue come up where you're not getting the full compensation to do the job and responsibilities you are asked for.

Do you see that with tribes? Do you think that is why there is some disparity with tribes on self-governance issues?

Mr. WASHBURN. Yes, Madam Chair. There are a lot of different views from the tribes out there about how we handle these issues. And we need to hear all of them before we decide.

10

The Appropriations Committee, their language that they are remanding the issue back to us to deal with, and that is the language
they put in the report. So we are trying to figure that out. We
know the tribes need contract support cost payments and we work
with the Indian Health Service because they face the same issue.
We have different challenges regarding these issues than the IHS
has, but we are trying to work with them at the request of tribes
and their counsel to make sure we coordinate with IHS as we address these issues. So we will be doing consultation with tribes to
figure out how to go forward, not just for this year, fiscal year
2014, but also as we prepare the FY 2015 budget, which is currently in process.

The CHAIRWOMAN. Do you think there are tribes that don't move
forward on self-governance because they are concerned about what
that means as far as compensation?

Mr. WASHBURN. Yes, Madam Chair. We actually think that once
it is clear that every tribe gets contract support costs, no questions,
that we are going to draw more tribes to self-governance because
they can count on that money. And so we have to plan for that, too.
So we are planning for that in our budget process, planning for the
notion that maybe there will be more tribes that are engaged in
self-governance, because they can now count on getting contract
support costs that they need to execute these contracts and operate
these contracts.

The CHAIRWOMAN. Thank you.

Vice Chairman Barrasso?

Senator BARRASSO. Thank you, good to see you again. I appreciate your being here.

The Department of the Interior administers a wide spectrum of
programs and projects that serve Indian communities. Section 202
of the bill contains limitations on modifying or affecting projects
not included in the Indian Self-Determination and Education Assistance Act, including water settlements.

So your testimony suggested that more work was needed on this
specific provision. I wonder what recommendations you might have
for us in terms of refining that provision.

Mr. WASHBURN. Thank you, Vice Chair. We are working with
your staff, Senate Committee staff, to try and figure out what that
language would be. The problem with the language is that different
lawyers read it to mean different things. We feel like we need to
get to clarity.

I think everybody agrees with the long-term intention, where we
are going with this. But if the lawyers can't all agree on what it
means, then we need to make it more clear. So we are working on
that.

So I don't have specific language for you, but our lawyers and
your lawyers are talking about trying to clarify that language.

Senator BARRASSO. I appreciate that. Just one last question. During the 111th Congress, in examining a prior but similar bill to
this, the Congressional Budget Office thought that implementation
would cost about a million dollars a year over five years. They indicated the department would use that extra million dollars for you
to hire additional staff, to make equipment upgrades.

Do you see the Administration believing that this additional funding is necessary?

Mr. WASHBURN. Vice Chair, I am not sure if it is necessary or not. But I will tell you, that is a fairly modest investment in what has been the most successful Federal Indian policy towards tribes ever in our history. So if that is the cost, I think it is something that we would be willing to bear.

We have a really wonderful Office of Self-Governance in the Indian Affairs area of Interior, run by Sharee Freeman, who is here with me today. She runs a very good staff, and we have actually just authorized her to hire two more staff because we need to be serving tribes better, we need to be getting money out quicker to tribes and that sort of thing under these compacts.

So that office frankly needs to grow a little bit more, probably, to help tribes get their appropriations, their money quicker, so that they can do the job better. And so we are doing a little bit of hiring in that area already.

I don't know exactly what the costs will be, but if there is a modest increase in investment, it is well worth it, I believe.

Senator BARRASSO. Thank you. Thank you, Madam Chairwoman.

The CHAIRWOMAN. Thank you. Senator Tester?

Senator TESTER. Thank you, Madam Chair.

Assistant Secretary Washburn, and I want to welcome the members on the next panel, one of which is Chairman Ron Trahan from the Confederated Salish and Kootenai Tribes of Montana. Thank you for making the long haul here, and we look forward to what you have to say.

Secretary Washburn, we have heard statements from tribal leaders that the BIA is more difficult to navigate when compared to IHS, when it comes to entering into contracts. Could you tell us how S. 919 may better enable the BIA to respond to the needs of tribal governments?

Mr. WASHBURN. I am not going to respond as to whether it is a fair criticism or not, except to note that the Indian Health Service has one function, one very important function, which is health care. And we have to do everything else, from water and irrigation to law enforcement to welfare assistance to housing to roads. It runs the gamut, education to realty.

So we bring different challenges to these issues. I do believe that S. 919 will make us function, the tribes prefer the way IHS functions to the way we function.

Senator TESTER. Correct.

Mr. WASHBURN. And this will make us function more like IHS does. And I think that is one of the things that really benefits the tribes, because there is some uniformity there. It is going to be more difficult than it is for IHS, because we have so many more different functions and different kinds of activities that we do.

But I think that it will, if it works better for tribes, ultimately it works better for us, because Federal Indian policy works better and the services get to the people better. So it is going to be a little bit more of a challenge to us, but we can live with that.

Senator TESTER. Okay. Looking at it from a tribal leadership standpoint, what kind of flexibility will S. 919 provide tribal leadership as tribes try to assert more home rule?

12

Mr. WASHBURN. One of the things it does is it puts much more of the onus on the Federal Government to act in a timely manner. It puts the onus on us to negotiate in good faith, which, there shouldn't have to be a law to say that when we negotiate we have to do it in good faith, but it will require that. So it doesn't matter who the Administration is, there will always be good faith negotiating or presumably a legal remedy if there is not.

So that is sort of the big thing that it helps with. It will require us to act in a much more timely way, which ultimately will get money to tribes quicker.

Senator TESTER. Beside supporting S. 919, what can you tell us that the Obama Administration is doing to help support more self-governance in Indian Country?

Mr. WASHBURN. Well, the FTEs that I talked about, we are increasing the size of that office. And frankly, part of the reason we are doing that is because Sharee Freeman, the director of that office, when I asked her how can we increase the number of tribes engaged in self-governance, she said, I need to get on the road. She said she needs to get on the road to talk to tribes and to get out to do some evangelizing, do some recruiting, basically. But her staff is so thin that she can't be away from the office to do that.

So she has also vowed to me that if I can get her more staff in the office, she will get out on the road to talk to more tribes to tell them the advantages of self-governance and ultimately we think that that will improve.

She has also been working really hard to improve training on self-governance issues. We have even sort of been looking at, in addition to S. 919, what is the next stage for self-governance? What does self-governance 2.0 look like? And Ms. Freeman has engaged the State Department to see, when we are providing aid to foreign countries, how does that work. We have been trying to be very creative in trying to figure out what the next development of self-governance should be.

Senator TESTER. Do you have the budgetary ability? In other words, do you have the dollars to bring some additional staff on?

Mr. WASHBURN. We are finding ways to accomplish that. Mostly stealing from Peter to pay Paul. But this is one of the most important things we do. So we need to find the staff to be able to fix it.

Senator TESTER. Sounds good. Thank you. I appreciate your work.

Mr. WASHBURN. Thank you.

The CHAIRWOMAN. Senator Murkowski?

Senator MURKOWSKI. Thank you, Madam Chairman.

Welcome, Dr. Washburn. I think you have the problem solved here in terms of how this Administration can do more when it comes to encouraging tribal self-governance. It goes back to the question that the Chairwoman asked in terms of full support for contract support costs. You mentioned that if tribes know that they can count on this, if they know that they are going to be reimbursed fully, if the uncertainty that they have seen is eliminated, I am not so convinced that you need to go on the road with a staff to try to sell it. I think it will sell itself.

But when you have uncertainty because you don't know whether you are going to get that reimbursement, if you think that that reimbursement is going to be 70 cents on the dollar, you are going to have tribes that are saying, I am going to sit back on this for a while.

So I would suggest that as you engage in the consultation, which I think is absolutely appropriate, that it be a very, very clear message to our tribes that the commitment that has been made is a commitment for full contract support costs, as the courts have directed, as the acts require. So I would certainly think that is how you answer the question of Senator Tester there in terms of what can be done.

I mentioned in my comments that there is a fair amount of disappointment in Alaska with the management of fish and wildlife and of public lands in the State. I have called for an expansion of these tribal self-governance agreements within our Federal agencies, specifically the national parks and national wildlife refuges. How do you feel about this? Do you think there is a role for these Federal agencies in working, whether it is with TCC or other tribes in terms of management of the lands in their areas?

Mr. WASHBURN. Yes, Madam Senator. I actually think that no one knows the lands better than the Alaska Natives do. So they can be trusted to help manage those lands themselves. We don't currently have trust lands in Alaska, so it is mostly other Federal lands. I think that we have to look to Alaska Natives to help us manage those lands, and they can do a good job. They are very competent, they know those lands well.

And especially at a time now where with climate change, those lands are changing, as the ice is changing dramatically. So I think that is right, I think there are a lot of institutions and organizations in Alaska that can do this job well.

Almost all of the Indian Health Service activity in Alaska, and maybe all of it, is contracted to tribes and tribal consortia. And they do a great job. So I think the other parts of the Federal Government should trust that they can work well with Alaska Natives.

Senator MURKOWSKI. What I think it is an important example to look to is what we have done on the health side. I think we have done a remarkable job. And it is these partnerships that have worked very effectively to the benefit of Alaska's native peoples when it comes to the health care. I think we can do more again when it comes to management of our public lands, and I would hope that our office would be working with us as we work to expand that.

Another issue that I have raised, and have asked for consideration by this Administration is ensuring that there is a place for Alaska Native residents on the Federal subsistence board, basically putting more subsistence users on that Federal subsistence board. What are your thoughts on that?

Mr. WASHBURN. I know that they looked at this board carefully in 2010, I believe, and suggested some changes to it. That was back when Secretary Salazar was in charge. And we do have, we have had Alaska Native leadership chairing the board. I think that is very important.

The board is mostly composed of land management agencies and then the BIA. We are not a land management agency currently in Alaska. Then we have the citizen members of the board, one of whom is Alaska Native and chairs the board. So I wouldn't presume to say what the final composition of the board should be, but I think that the board's work is very, very important and Alaska Natives need to have a strong voice, because that is really who the board serves.

Senator MURKOWSKI. I would ask you to take a look at that as an issue as well as the rural determination process. There is of course a great deal of concern that this process for determining whether or not a village is rural or not is a fair and adequate process. I have asked for review of that, too. So several things I think we can be working on to try to ensure that when it comes to Alaska Natives and tribal self-governance, self-determination that we are really fulfilling that intent to the maximum extent.

Just one last thing. As you know, I was extremely, extremely disappointed in Secretary of the Interior's decision as it related to King Cove. I felt that the report that was made public by you after your visit was inadequate and did not adequately address the trust responsibility that I believe the DOI has to Alaska Native residents there in King Cove. So I would ask that we set up a meeting in my office or I will come to your office so we can discuss this further. If we can do it before the President's Day recess, I would appreciate any consideration you would give. I am sorry to put you on the spot and I don't expect you to answer me as to when we can do it, but I would like to have that sit-down with you.

Mr. WASHBURN. I would be happy to make that a priority, Senator Murkowski. The trust responsibility, I understand your position, let me just say that I did get to weigh in, and weighed in very strongly after hearing from the community of King Cove. I think the trust responsibility is something that we share, the Congress and the Executive Branch share. So I would push back a little bit, because if the Congress had made more clear what the trust responsibility means in that context, it might have produced a different result. But we certainly have a trust responsibility too, and I am happy to talk more about that.

Senator MURKOWSKI. I look forward to that visit. Thank you, Madam Chair.

The CHAIRWOMAN. Senator Begich?

STATEMENT OF HON. MARK BEGICH,
U.S. SENATOR FROM ALASKA

Senator BEGICH. Thank you very much, Madam Chair. I wasn't here at the beginning, but I first want to say, from my limited time on here so far, thank you for the role you have played as Chair of the Committee. I greatly appreciate the guidance you have given me as a new member on the Committee. So thank you for everything you have been able to do here.

Let me also say, I am not sure what my time will be, but to Jerry, I may be here, I may not be, but I want to say thank you for coming all the way from Alaska. It is always good to have Alaskans here, where it is colder here than there, which is hard to explain to people. When I got a photo today of green grass in Anchorage, you have to wonder what is going on. So I appreciate your being here.

I think we all agree that S. 919 is an important piece of legislation. But I want to cut to a couple of pieces, and again, always good to see you and be able to ask you a few questions and kind of follow up on what some other members have talked about. Obviously contract support costs are always on our mind. I think BIA is moving forward, I think the court has ruled and you are moving forward on settlement issues.

But the challenge is this, I guess, when you look at the court's ruling, at least in the case that when they ruled they said between fiscal year 1994 and 2001, appropriations covered only between 77 and 92 percent of the tribe's aggregated contract support costs. So it begs the question, and it will lead to my larger question, and that is, if we know what you paid and we know what you haven't paid, because it is a mathematical issue here, but it seems based on the timetables that it will take to settle some of these issues, it could take a couple of years.

The question I have for you is the shortfall reports that are given to Congress annually, which in theory, and you can correct me if I am wrong here, the shortfall reports say here is what we are falling short in paying. In theory those are factual, based on data, so we know if you paid X and the shortfall report says this, then that is what is owed. So why is it going to take so long to settle these when we know what is owed? Because I can only assume those reports are correct. Because those were submitted to Congress.

So help me understand this dilemma, because what I keep hearing from folks as well, they want to re-examine what the costs really were. But then I would argue if that is the case, the shortfall reports were useless. But they are shortfall reports. And the court then says, here is what has been paid, so it seems like a simple math problem, then pay what is owed. Help me understand that.

Mr. WASHBURN. Thank you, Senator Begich. And I won't do that.

Senator BEGICH. But I need you to do that.

[Laughter.]

Senator WASHBURN. It is fairly complicated. Let me just say this. When we report an aggregate shortfall report, it doesn't say how much each tribe is owed. So that is a big aggregate.

Senator BEGICH. Let me pause you there. But you then agree the total amount in those reports is what is short, what is owed? You just said that, right?

Mr. WASHBURN. Well, I don't know if that is, this is a matter in litigation so I am on thin ice here. I will get in trouble whatever I say, basically.

Senator BEGICH. There is thick ice in D.C., there is thin ice in Alaska right now.

[Laughter.]

Mr. WASHBURN. Let me say this. At the BIA we are working through a process with plaintiffs' counsel to statistically sample. There is a big question about whether the tribes have to prove up their actual expenditures or not. And there is a big debate about that. The tribes say, well, we didn't necessarily have actual expenditures, because we didn't get the money to spend. And that is a fair point. But under ordinary Federal contracting law, if you can't show that you incurred a cost, then you can't get reimbursement for that cost, I gather. And I am probably oversimplifying things, but these are the ways I understand this.

I will tell you that I think S. 919 will help solve this problem going forward, because it will make really clear which Federal contracting laws apply to tribes and which don't.

Senator BEGICH. I appreciate that, but I guess my point is, and I know you are trying to figure out and describe this in the public arena when we are in litigation issues. But can I ask you this, then, can you submit to me or to the Committee, whatever would be the appropriate channel, but I would like to get a more definitive timetable of how you are going to settle these. Because my worry is that these will just go on and on and on. The Supreme Court has ruled, we know the amounts, or we know the potential aggregate.

Then I would like a comment at some point, not necessarily now but in writing, if you don't agree with the total aggregate in their shortfall reports, in other words, at the end of the day, if we settle with tribes and it is this much money based on those reports, then that should be easy. But if you are saying those may not be the right numbers, then we have to figure out why those reports are being submitted and what is the better way to approach this.

Because really, first off, we never want to see those reports, because you should be paying 100 percent. But I am a little perplexed by that. Because when we see those reports, we assume this is what is owed. But if you are saying that is not exactly right, there are some variances, then that makes me, especially as an appropriator, a little wondering what is going on there. So you have to help me there. You don't have to do it now, but if you can kind of think about that issue.

Then the last, and if this puts you on the spot you don't have to answer it. But I just want to follow up on what Senator Murkowski said, especially about King Cove. I sensed, the comment you made is if the Congress had defined the trust relationship differently, the outcome may have been different. What did you mean by that? And why I say that is because, did you have a different opinion on those conversations on King Cove? And if you don't want to answer, I understand. But I sense that there might have been some differences here, and if there is, what were they? Then second, what do we have to change to give you that authority if the outcome will be different. I think that is kind of the goal.

Mr. WASHBURN. Senator Murkowski met with me before I went to King Cove and very clearly asked me to look at sort of the trust responsibility implications of what we were doing, and her staff. We met with a lot of her staff and her staff were very thoughtful. So I looked at the statute, and it was part of an omnibus statute, this portion about Isenbeck and King Cove. The omnibus statute had several provisions. It was a big public lands act.

Senator BEGICH. Public lands went in 2009.

Mr. WASHBURN. That is right. And the trust responsibility was discussed in other places with regard to tribes. But the trust responsibility was not mentioned once with regard to the King Cove community at Isenbeck. It is Congress that first defines the trust responsibility. It is up to you, it is up to Congress to say what does the trust responsibility mean in any given context.

So that is what I found when I looked. When I looked at what does the trust responsibility mean here, I learned that we had no guidance from Congress whatsoever on that point. It is Congress' duty in the first instance to define the trust responsibility.

We certainly have a trust responsibility, too. Executive Branch bears that responsibility. But it is formally defined by Congress, and Congress has plenary authority over Indian Affairs. So if it is defined by Congress, we have to follow that. It was utterly absent in that statute.

So I would invite you the next time, if you want to make sure you get this done, you talk specifically about the trust responsibility to King Cove. This is a difficult issue. There are strong feelings on both sides of it. The Secretary I don't think was happy to be in the position of having to make this very difficult decision, which places very important values against one another. And I am frankly sorry to have to be in a position to make decisions like that. These are the hardest decisions we make. Because they make a real difference in people's lives and lots of people care about them.

So that is what I was getting at.

Senator BEGICH. Thank you very much. And as always, you are great on testimony. Thank you for always coming to Alaska.

Mr. WASHBURN. Thank you.

The CHAIRWOMAN. Thank you, and again, Assistant Secretary Washburn, thank you for being here. I don't think that any of us conspired with our staff to make this all about contract support. I think it is just a natural continuation of our quest to make sure that this issue is rectified. Both of my colleagues, Senator Murkowski and Senator Begich, invited me to Alaska this summer and I went. I have to say that the Alaska Native Medical Center is a state of the art facility, not just in Indian Country, but in the entire United States. They deserve their contract support and they are leading the way, juxtaposed to an IHS-run facility that is not necessarily innovating, meeting the needs of the community. So those are the two paths and choices, move toward the kind of innovation that is being delivered in Indian Country and in self-governance. So we really have to rectify this issue.

But I just wanted you to know, I don't think we all conspired, it is just a natural outflow. This is part of this discussion of self-governance and it is the complaints and concerns that we have heard before. I am sure the next panel is going to tell us a lot about just the day to day details of the success of self-governance. But we have to get this larger issue out from hanging over the self-governance issue.

Again, thank you for being here.

Mr. WASHBURN. It is my honor. Thank you.

The CHAIRWOMAN. So we will hear now from our second panel of witnesses, as I have introduced them previously. We are so thankful for them being here.

Ron Allen from the Jamestown S'Klallam Tribe; the Honorable Ron Trahan from the Salish Kootenai Tribes of Montana; Jerry Isaac, from the Tanana Chiefs Conference of Fairbanks, Alaska; and Mr. Mickey Peercy, Executive Director for Self-Governance for the Choctaw Nation.

We are going to start with you, Mr. Allen. Again, thank you for being here, thank you for your leadership on the self-governance issue overall.

STATEMENT OF HON. W. RON ALLEN, CHAIRMAN/CEO, JAMESTOWN S'KLALLAM TRIBE

Mr. ALLEN. Thank you, Madam Chair.

It is always an honor and a privilege to come before this Committee to testify on behalf of any legislation that affects the welfare and the interest of Indian Country, and my tribe specifically. I do want to say that I am disappointed to hear that you are moving on as the Chair. You have done a great job on behalf of Indian Country and we are very proud of you, coming from Washington State, knowing the 29 tribes of Washington State, that you know our issues and you know the issues of Indian Country.

I know it is almost like drinking from a fire hose when you deal with the complex issues of Indian Country, from Alaska to Florida. Senator Tester, I am glad to hear that you are going to step in. I know you are a great champion as well. And Senator Murkowski as well, on the Republican side, you have been a staunch supporter of Indian Country and our sovereignty. And we deeply appreciate your leadership as well.

I am here to testify on behalf of S. 919. This is the culmination of a long negotiation between the tribes and the Congress and the Administration. It is a bill that has a lot of blood, sweat and tears written all over it. I want to thank you and your staff on both sides of the aisle who have worked very hard for us, with us, to make this thing happen. Assistant Secretary Washburn and his staff have been deeply engaged with us.

For the most part, on the BIA side, those issues were worked out a long time ago. The heart of the matter ended up being more on the non-BIA side in clarifying some issues that you will see identified in Section 202.

But the bottom line is that this this bill brings Title 4 in line with Title 5. It continues on with the empowerment of tribal governments. I want to pause here and say, just the backdrop of our history in America and the family of governments, Indian governments were the first governments before this Union was even formed. We are recognized in the Constitution.

So it took a lot of generations and a lot of years for the true relationship between Indian governments and the United States and the sister governments throughout America to have a respectful relationship to advance the interests of Indian Country and all the people that we serve.

This bill is about that. It is about empowering tribal governments. Yes, it affects all of our programs, natural resources, law enforcement, education and so forth. And that is our duty, just like it is your duty to serve all of America and all of its interests. We just happen to be smaller, including our largest tribe, the Navajo Nation, that now is venturing into self-governance as well.

So as you noted, there are well over half the tribes now that are in self-governance and moving forward. This bill is going to help make that happen. It is going to clean up the relationship. It is going to improve the process. It is going to clarify the relationship with regard to construction projects that are in place.

And last but not least, it is going to make sure that it protects the administrative responsibilities with regard to non-BIA programs and with regard to legislation that affects water rights issues, as complex as they may be, throughout Indian Country. That was one of the tough issues that we had to deal with, and we think that we have worked out some language that addresses that issue and protects the interests of both the tribes and the interests of the Administration as it carries out its responsibilities in that mater.

Self-governance really, when I reflect back, I was at the first hearing in 1987, as a result of the exposes that came out of the fraud, abuse, misuse of Federal funds. And ended up culminating in self-governance and the approval of Title 4 in 1994. A fascinating experience, and it has been a fascinating experience ever since then. It is an unequivocal success, the flexibility, the ability for us to take these very limited Federal resources and use them more efficiently and more effectively to address our communities, as this is the success of self-governance. It is the empowerment, it is the trust between the United States and the Indian governments and our leadership that we know how to use these resources, consistent with their intent and as they were applied to our people.

It doesn't always work, one size fit all, Washington, D.C., you folks certainly know that. This allows us to be able to tailor it to tribe in Montana, tribes in Washington, tribes in Alaska and so forth across Indian Country. That flexibility that Kevin Washburn referred to, the strengthening of our planning and management issues, affirming of our tribal sovereignty is a critical issue that definitely helps us move our agenda forward.

It is not perfect. It doesn't address all of our issues. But it does move the agenda forward, it moves it forward constructively, and I think as a result of it, as you have asked earlier in opening remarks and that dialogue with Assistant Secretary Washburn, that is it going to result in more tribes getting engaged with the self-governance process and forum.

I think that it is important to know that it allows us to use these resources to leverage other resources, including Federal resources that we weren't able to do before. If tribes don't have resources to leverage other Federal resources, sometimes they don't have an option and opportunity. This provides them that option and that opportunity.

Final offer, and some of the provisions that are in my testimony, and you can review them at your pleasure, will show the different steps that allow us to improve the negotiations. Part of the problems, sometimes tribes can't find out what is their fair share of a program A, B and C. They need to identify that so they are comfortable and that people are comfortable that they can take over that program and administer it in the interest of the tribe and the people that they serve.

I will conclude with, this is an important chapter we are turning. I really hope that we can move this legislation forward, that the House has a complementary piece of legislation and that this year we can finally see Title 4 be consistent with Title 5.

Thank you, Madam Chair.
[The prepared statement of Mr. Allen follows:]

PREPARED STATEMENT OF HON. W. RON ALLEN, CHAIRMAN/CEO, JAMESTOWN
S'KLALLAM TRIBE

Good afternoon. Thank you for the opportunity to be here today to testify once again on this critical legislation. My name is W. Ron Allen and I am the Chairman/CEO of the Jamestown S'Klallam Tribe located in Washington State. I am also the Chairman of the Department of the Interior (DOI) Self-Governance Advisory Committee (SGAC), and I offer my testimony today in both capacities. Collectively, I am representing well over 300 Tribes that participate in Self-Governance within DOI and the Department of Health and Human Services (HHS), Indian Health Service (IHS).

I am pleased to testify in support of S. 919, a bill to strengthen Indian Tribes' opportunities for Self-Governance by amending Title IV of the Indian Self-Determination and Education Assistance Act (ISDEAA) (P.L. 93–638, as amended). The proposed Title IV amendments advance three basic goals:

- To bring Title IV up to par with Title V, the permanent Self-Governance authority within HHS;
- To clean up the construction provisions of Title IV; and
- To maintain unchanged the discretionary authority to enter Self-Governance agreements with non-BIA agencies in Interior.

Before expanding on the need for these critical amendments, I will talk briefly about the success of the Self-Governance policy over the past 20 years and the Tribal-federal collaboration to expand that success through the Title IV amendments.

The Success of Self-Governance

The increasing number of Tribes that have opted to participate in the Self-Governance program on an annual basis reflects the success of the program. In Fiscal Year 1991, the first year Self-Governance agreements were negotiated by the BIA with Tribes, only seven Tribes entered into agreements. At that time, the total dollar amount compacted by Indian Tribes was $27.1 million. By Fiscal Year 2013, 254 Tribes and Tribal consortia entered into 106 funding agreements, operating $432 million in programs, functions, services and activities. [1] The growth in Tribal participation in Self-Governance revealed by these numbers reflects the success of the program. Under Self-Governance, Tribes have assumed the management of a large number of DOI programs, including roads, housing, education, law enforcement, court systems, and natural resources management. Why? Simply put, Self-Governance works.

- *Self-Governance Promotes Efficiency.* Devolving federal administration from Washington, D.C. to Indian Tribes across the United States has strengthened the efficient management and delivery of federal programs impacting Indian Tribes. As this Committee well knows, prior to Self-Governance, up to 90 percent of federal funds earmarked for Indian Tribes were used by federal agencies for administrative purposes. Under Self-Governance, program responsibility and accountability has shifted from distant federal personnel to elected Tribal leaders. In turn, program efficiency has increased as politically accountable Tribal leaders leverage their knowledge of local resources, conditions and trends to make cost-saving management decisions.
- *Self-Governance Strengthens Tribal Planning and Management Capacities.* By placing Tribes in decisionmaking positions, Self-Governance vests Tribes with ownership of the critical ingredient necessary to plan our own futures—information. At the same time, Self-Governance has provided a generation of Tribal members with management experience beneficial for the continued effective stewardship of our resources.
- *Self-Governance Allows for Flexibility.* Self-Governance allows Tribes great flexibility when making decisions concerning allocation of funds. Whether managing programs in a manner consistent with traditional values or allocating funds to meet changing priorities, Self-Governance Tribes are developing in ways consistent with their own needs and priorities, not a monolithic federal policy.

---

[1] Source: Dep't of the Interior, *Budget Justifications and Performance Information, FY 2014, Indian Affairs,* Appendix 7.

- *Self-Governance Affirms Sovereignty.* By utilizing signed compacts, Self-Governance affirms the fundamental government-to-government relationship between Indian Tribes and the U.S. Government. It also advances a political agenda of both the Congress and the Administration: namely, shifting federal functions to local governmental control.

In short, Self-Governance works, because it places management responsibility in the hands of those who care most about seeing Indian programs succeed: Indian Tribes and their members.

Need for Title IV Amendments

As important and successful as the Self-Governance initiative has been for my Tribe and so many others, it is not perfect. Shortly after Title IV was enacted in 1994, the DOI began a rulemaking process to develop and promulgate regulations. The process was a failure in many ways. Ultimately, five years after the rulemaking process began, DOI published regulations that, from the Tribal perspective, failed to fully implement Congress's intent when Title IV was enacted. Instead of moving the initiative forward, it moved backwards.

Tribal leaders began discussions about how the statute could be amended. At the same time, Congress in 2000 enacted Title V of the ISDEAA which created a permanent Self-Governance program within HHS, and which directly addressed many of the issues that proved to be problematic during the Title IV rulemaking process. But many of the improvements and Tribal authority reflected in Title V remain absent from Title IV. Consequently, many Self-Governance Tribes are forced to operate under two separate sets of administrative requirements, one for IHS and one for BIA.

Tribal leaders decided that Title IV needed to be amended to incorporate many of Title V's provisions. It has long been a top legislative priority of Tribal leaders to amend Title IV. In the last ten years, I have testified several times before this Committee in support of predecessor bills to S. 919.[2] Some members of Congress may be tired of hearing from me on this issue, but our persistence speaks to the importance Tribal leadership has placed on amending Title IV with respect to empowering Tribal governance to manage limited federal resources to benefit Tribal citizens.

S. 919 reflects over ten years of discussions, drafting, negotiation, and redrafting. Particularly in the past two years, Tribal representatives, along with agency and Congressional staff, have worked hard to come up with a bill that everyone can support. The time has come to pass this legislation, which would significantly advance Congress's policy of promoting Tribal Self-Governance for American Indian and Alaska Native Tribal governments.

Overview of S. 919

The proposed bill will bring Title IV into line with Title V, creating administrative efficiencies for Tribes while also importing the beneficial provisions of Title V currently missing in the older Self-Governance statute. Let me quickly summarize a few of the key provisions in S. 919. To address problems in the DOI's implementation of the Tribal Self-Governance program, S. 919 would, among other things:

- conform Title IV to Title V in order to create consistency and administrative efficiencies for Tribes now operating under two compacting regimes;
- establish a clear "final offer" process and timelines for situations when DOI and the Tribe are unable to agree on particular terms of a compact or funding agreement, or when DOI delays approval unreasonably;
- clarify and limit the reasons for which the agency may decline to enter a proposed agreement;
- protect Tribes from DOI attempts to impose unauthorized terms in compacts or funding agreements;
- provide a clear avenue of appeal and burden of proof for Tribes to challenge adverse agency decisions;
- clarify Tribal and federal oversight roles in construction to ensure fiscal prudence and public safety;
- leave unchanged the discretionary authority to compact non-BIA programs within DOI; and

---

[2] *E.g.*, SCIA Hearing on H.R. 4347, Department of the Interior Tribal Self-Governance Act of 2010 (Nov. 18, 2010); SCIA Oversight Hearing on the Success and Shortfall of Self-Governance under the Indian Self-Determination and Education Assistance Act after Twenty Years (May 13, 2008).

• make important amendments to Title I, the self-determination contracting law, such as clarifying reporting requirements, rules of interpretation, and applicability of certain Title I provisions to Title IV agreements.

There is ample precedent for most of S. 919 in Title V, which has worked very well in the context of health care services and served as the model for this legislation. Tribes have already conceded on very significant key issues-for example, removing provisions on mandatory compacting of non-BIA programs. The fundamental principles guiding S. 919 are all sound, as proven by the success of Title V over the last decade.

Conclusion

The Title IV amendments embodied in S. 919 significantly advance the U.S. policy of Tribal Self-Governance. These amendments would cost nothing; indeed, they would promote the efficient use of federal funds and improve services to Tribal communities across the nation. The legislation enjoys broad support among Tribes and their friends in Congress and Interior. S. 919 is the product of almost 14 years of experience, discussion, and compromise. Now is the time for this Committee, and Congress as a whole, to push the bill forward so we can build on the impressive success of the past and further Tribal Self-Governance, in partnership with the United States, to improve the lives of our Tribal citizens.

Thank you for this opportunity to share our views on this important legislative initiative for our Tribe and Indian Country.

The CHAIRWOMAN. Thank you, and thanks again for traveling all this way. Now we will hear from Chairman Trahan. Thank you for being here.

STATEMENT OF HON. RONALD TRAHAN, CHAIRMAN, CONFEDERATED SALISH AND KOOTENAI TRIBES

Mr. TRAHAN. Thank you. I will read my statement out here, so it is my testimony, so bear with me if you would, please.

Good afternoon, Chairwoman Cantwell, Senator Tester and Committee members. My name is Ron Trahan. I am serving as the newly elected Tribal Chairman of the Salish and Kootenai Tribes of Montana.

I also want to thank you personally, Chairwoman Cantwell, for the time that you spent with us on the Flathead Indian Reservation back in September, when you were visiting with Senator Tester.

I will keep my remarks brief, since you have my written testimony.

The Confederated Salish and Kootenai Tribes support S. 919, as well as the proposed changes to the bill under Committee consideration. As discussed in my written testimony, my tribe has a long history with self-governance contracting. Our late chairman, Ricky Pablo, was a tireless advocate for the adoption of self-governance laws. It does my heart good to report our tribes have thrived under the laws we helped enact.

Ricky and former Chairman of the Committee, Senator Inouye, were great partners. We owe a great debt of gratitude to them and also former Vice Chair McCain and the many other tribal and Congressional leaders who turned self-governance into reality. Due in part to our extensive contracting activities and in part to our commercial activities by tribes, our tribe is the largest employer in northwest Montana and one of the largest in western Montana. The Confederated Salish and Kootenai government alone has over 1,000 full-time employees. Currently the tribal government annually administers approximately $25 million in self-governance

23

funds, $150 million in contracts and grants and $45 million in tribal revenue.

A repot funded by the State of Montana several years ago showed that the Confederated Salish and Kootenai Tribes contributed $317 million to the Montana economy annually. Thanks in part to self-governance policies, we are a key player in building our reservation's and regional economies.

As with our prior testimony on this legislation in past Congresses, I would like to update you on our self-governance efforts at the National Bison Range and Complex. I refer to the complex not just the National Bison Range, because the complex includes not only the bison range but two additional wild refuges that are located on tribally owned land, which is the Ninepipe and Pablo National Refuge.

As you may know, we have been working for almost 20 years to secure a stable funding agreement with the U.S. Fish and Wildlife Service for the programs at the Bison Range complex. In 2008, our tribe signed an agreement with the service that allowed them to have a meaningful role in the operations of the bison range. That signing ceremony at the Interior Department was attended by Senator Baucus, Senator Tester and Secretary Kempthorne, among others.

Over the next two years, that parties were very satisfied with the partnership. The agreement was challenged in Federal court by a group who opposed the tribal presence at the Bison range. The court rescinded the agreement on procedural grounds under the National Environmental Policy Act. We have been trying ever since to deal with the technicalities and return to the Bison Range. My written testimony gives a more detailed overview of the most recent history.

The Fish and Wildlife Service is currently working on an environmental assessment of our new draft agreement. Yesterday we met and discussed our efforts with Dan Ashe, the Director of Fish and Wildlife Service. He assured me that the service wants to return to the productive partnership they had with us at the Bison Range and Complex. The partnership success we had with the Bison Rang is one reason why groups like the National Wildlife Federation supports the tribe's return under a new self-governance agreement.

While we are frustrated by the amount of time it is taking for us to return to the bison range, it is our hope that the partnership we have built with the services at both field and policy maker levels will continue, and that this will happen sooner rather than later. We have exercised great patience over the last 20 years, but it simply should not take this long.

Our bison range partnership will once again benefit the Service, the tribes and the communities, making the self-governance agreement in everyone's best interest. We appreciate the support that this Committee and others in Congress have shown for our efforts.

In concluding my remarks, the tribes support S. 919. Thank you again for the opportunity to share my thoughts with you. I also extend a personal invitation to the Chairwoman, Vice Chairman and all members of this Committee to visit the beautiful Flathead In-

24

dian Reservation so we can share with you more of what we do and who we are.

At this time I would, along with my staff, happily try to answer any questions that you have. And again, thank you.

[The prepared statement of Mr. Trahan follows:]

PREPARED STATEMENT OF HON. RONALD TRAHAN, CHAIRMAN, CONFEDERATED SALISH AND KOOTENAI TRIBES

Greetings Chairwoman Cantwell, Vice-Chairman Barrasso, Senator Tester and Committee members. My name is Ron Trahan and I serve as the Chairman of the Confederated Salish and Kootenai Tribes ("CSKT" or "Tribes").

On behalf of the Confederated Salish and Kootenai Tribes, I thank you for the opportunity to provide our views on S. 919, including proposed revisions to the bill that are under Committee consideration. CSKT supports the legislation.

This legislation, which would amend the Tribal Self-Governance Act's Interior Department provisions, found in Title IV of the Indian Self-Determination and Education Assistance Act (ISDEAA), has a long history. Ten years ago, in 2004, one of my predecessors, Chairman D. Fred Matt, testified before this Committee on an earlier version of S. 919 (S.1715). Seven years ago, in 2007, another of my predecessors, James Steele, Jr., also testified here on draft legislation to amend the Tribal Self-Governance Act.

The success and resilience of the Tribal Self-Governance Act, and Self-Governance tribes, is unquestioned. The record of success built by Self-Governance tribes is a testament to the foresight and wisdom of tribal and congressional leaders. The late CSKT Chairman Michael ("Mickey") T. Pablo, had fiercely fought for enactment of Tribal Self-Governance legislation and policies. As we have stated before, the record built by CSKT, and Indian country, in administering federal programs would make Mickey proud. Mickey was instrumental in CSKT becoming one of the first ten tribes in the country to participate in the Tribal Self-Governance Demonstration Project in the late 1980's, and he was a key player in the subsequent permanent establishment of Tribal Self-Governance as federal policy.

I would also like to acknowledge the essential contributions of this Committee, and its leadership under former Co-Chairmen Daniel K. Inouye and John McCain, in establishing Tribal Self-Governance as permanent federal policy. The manner in which Congress worked with tribal leaders to develop, test, and then permanently enact the Tribal Self-Governance paradigm is an outstanding model for how policy should be formulated.

CSKT has long asserted that ISDEA and its 1994 amendments, known as the Tribal Self-Governance Act (Title IV of ISDEAA), have been two of the most important and successful pieces of federal Indian legislation in history. They are a logical progression from the Indian Reorganization Act of 1934, which first set the stage under federal law for tribal governments to once again determine our own affairs, protect our own communities, and provide for our own people in concert with our respective cultures and traditions—something we have done since time immemorial. Fully implementing Tribal Self-Governance is a pivotal step in realizing the federal policy of Indian Self-Determination that was ushered in almost forty years ago.

CSKT's Self-Governance Background

General Background

CSKT has been one of the most active of the many Self-Governance tribes and, as mentioned above, is one of the original ten Self-Governance tribes. We have found the system of Self-Governance contracting, through compacts and annual funding agreements (AFA's), to be highly effective in: (1) increasing the efficiency and integrity of federal services to tribes and tribal members; (2) increasing tribal autonomy and self-sufficiency; (3) strengthening the government-to-government relationship between the United States and tribal governments; and (4) developing our Tribal economy. All of these are among the principal objectives identified by Congress in its policy rationale for ISDEAA:

> [T]he United States is committed to supporting and assisting Indian tribes in the development of strong and stable tribal governments, capable of administering quality programs and developing the economies of their respective communities.

25 U.S.C. §450a(b)

As Congress later stated in enacting the Tribal Self-Governance Act of 1994:

The Tribal right of self-government flows from the inherent sovereignty of Indian tribes and nations[. . . .] It is the policy of the Tribal Self-Governance Act to permanently establish and implement self-governance . . . [t]o permit each Tribe to choose the extent of its participation in self-governance.

25 C.F.R. § 1000.4(a)(1), (b)(2)

Currently, the CSKT Tribal government annually administers approximately: $25 million in Self-Governance funds; $150 million in contracts and grants; and $44 million in Tribal revenue. Our government alone has 1,000 full-time employees. We are the largest employer on the Flathead Reservation, the largest employer in northwestern Montana, and we contribute over $30 million in payroll and over $50 million in purchasing to the local economy. A report funded by the State of Montana several years ago showed that CSKT contributed $317 million to the Montana economy annually.[1] It is important to remember, however, that the Indian unemployment rate on our Reservation is still much higher than that of the general area population. This is an indicator that we have a long way to go in building our Tribal and Reservation economies. To this end, the Tribal Self-Governance Act remains a vital tool for us.

The following is a list of just several examples of CSKT's successes in administering programs through ISDEAA and Self-Governance:

- In 1986, we signed a contract to take over control and management of the electrical utility on our reservation, then known as the Electrical Division of the Flathead Indian Irrigation Project. We renamed it Mission Valley Power (MVP). This utility serves every home and business on the reservation, Indians and non-Indians alike. It also provides power to the National Bison Range. It is considered one of the best-run utilities in the state of Montana. Since the Tribes took over, MVP has replaced and updated much of the utility's infrastructure yet managed to retain some of the lowest rates in the region. MVP has been 638-contracted and has not been included in subsequent Self-Governance agreements due to the prohibition found in 25 U.S.C. § 458cc(b)(4)(C). CSKT supports S. 919's deletion of this prohibition.

- Since 1996, CSKT has contracted the operation of the Bureau of Indian Affairs' (BIA) Land Title Recording Office (LTRO) for the Flathead Indian Reservation. We are aware of only a few other tribes that contract or compact the LTRO program in its entirety. Through Tribal control, we have: greatly decreased waiting time for requested documents; more nimbly adjusted priorities to respond to different needs regarding appraisals, mortgages, leases, etc.; and increased budget efficiencies for a program that is severely underfunded by the federal government. Tribal operation of LTRO functions has also been a key factor in CSKT's record of proactive land acquisitions and reduction of land fractionation through Tribal acquisition of fractionated interests.

- In 1989, CSKT contracted the BIA's Safety of Dams (SOD) program. One of the main objectives of this program is to eliminate or remediate structural and/or safety concerns at 17 locations on the Flathead Indian Reservation as identified by the Department of Interior National Dams—Technical Priority Rating listing. CSKT's SOD Program provides investigations, designs and SOD modifications to resolve the concerns of the dams on the list. The Tribes' SOD Program has been extremely successful and, under our administration, Reservation dams have been modified at a cost significantly lower than originally estimated by the Bureau of Reclamation. Past examples include completion of Black Lake Dam in November 1992 at a savings of approximately $1.3 million below Bureau of Reclamation estimates. The Pablo Dam Modification Project was completed in February 1994 at a savings of nearly $140,000.

- In fiscal years 1997 and 1998 respectively, CSKT began compacting for administration of the Individual Indian Monies (IIM) program for the Flathead Reservation. As of the January 23, 2013 *Federal Register* listing of Tribal Self-Governance agreements with non-BIA agencies, CSKT is the only tribe that currently has such an agreement with the Office of Special Trustee (OST) for these functions.

---

[1] "Monetary Contributions of Reservations to the State of Montana", prepared by Eleanor YellowRobe, Bureau of Business and Economic Research, University of Montana (submitted to State Tribal Economic Development Commission, Montana Department of Commerce—November 2007) pp. 1, 9–10.

National Bison Range Complex

With respect to non-BIA programs, the Interior Department has not established a very encouraging record regarding Tribal Self-Governance agreements. As this Committee is well aware, for almost twenty years CSKT has been working to secure a stable funding agreement with the U.S. Fish & Wildlife Service (FWS) for programs at the National Bison Range Complex (NBRC), which is almost entirely located within the Flathead Indian Reservation. The NBRC includes two ancillary National Wildlife Refuges that are located on Tribally-owned land in the center of the Reservation (the Ninepipe and Pablo Refuges).

While the effort has been unnecessarily expensive, frustrating and resource-intensive, it is worth the fight. In addition to the National Bison Range's physical location in the center of our Reservation, the NBRC's bison herd has its origins with the bison herd started and grown by Tribal members in the late 1800's and early 1900's, when bison were threatened with extinction. The NBRC's Ninepipe and Pablo Refuges are the result of Tribal requests in the 1910's and 1920's for the federal government to put the areas around two irrigation reservoirs into protected status for bird conservation. After several years, the United States responded by issuing two Executive Orders designating the areas as Refuges. In 1948, Congress acquired a perpetual easement from CSKT for such Refuge uses at Ninepipe and Pablo, while also recognizing the Tribes' reserved rights on the properties. [2] Collectively, the National Bison Range and the Ninepipe and Pablo Refuges occupy a unique place within our Reservation, our history, our culture, and our hearts.

As this Committee is aware, the CSKT has executed two multi-year AFA's with FWS for programs at the NBRC. The first AFA was signed in 2004, and the second was signed in 2008 at a Washington, D.C. ceremony attended by Interior Secretary Dirk Kempthorne and Montana Senators Jon Tester and Max Baucus. Unfortunately, both of these agreements came to premature ends.

With the negotiation and implementation of the 2008 AFA for NBRC programs, which covered fiscal years 2009–2011, CSKT and FWS built a highly constructive relationship both on the ground and at the policy-maker level. That relationship was reflected in many ways, including: positive status reports; successful annual bison round-ups; positive visitor feedback; and increased general communication and coordination between federal and tribal staffs.

Unfortunately, two non-governmental organizations [3] who have consistently opposed the federal-tribal partnership, challenged the agreement in a federal court action, stating that it violated a number of federal statutes such as the Tribal Self-Governance Act and the National Wildlife Refuge System Administration Act. The court did not rule on any of those substantive claims, but it did find that FWS failed to properly explain its invocation of a categorical exclusion under the National Environmental Policy Act when it approved the AFA, so the court rescinded the agreement on the basis of that procedural violation. The court decision was handed down in September 2010. In the three and a half years since that decision, CSKT has negotiated a new draft agreement with FWS and the agency then began preparing an Environmental Assessment for the draft agreement. It is still in the process of preparing that Assessment.

CSKT is pleased to have a wide pool of support for an NBRC Self-Governance agreement, including from conservation groups such as the National Wildlife Federation (*see* attached letter from NWF submitted in response to FWS' 2012 request for scoping comments regarding the Environmental Assessment). As stated by then-Chairman and Ranking Member of the House Natural Resources Committee, Congressmen Nick Rahall and Don Young:

> Working with Tribal governments . . . under the authorization of the Tribal Self-Governance Act should not be viewed any differently than partnering with State governments especially in this instance where the tribe owns the land on which the ancillary facilities of the NBRC National Bison Range Complex [*sic*] are located. [4]

While we have been very frustrated with the length of time that this process is taking, we are hopeful that the improved relationship between CSKT and FWS will result in a satisfactory agreement that will return CSKT staff to the National Bison Range soon so we can continue what was widely-acknowledged to be an effective partnership. As the *New York Times* said in a September 3, 2003 editorial address-

---

[2] Act of May 25, 1948, 62 Stat. 269, at Section 5(b).

[3] Public Employees for Environmental Responsibility (PEER) and the Blue Goose Alliance.

[4] May 15, 2007 letter to Interior Secretary Dirk Kempthorne from House Natural Resources Committee Chairman Nick Rahall and Ranking Minority Member Don Young, p. 2 (copy attached to this testimony).

ing the Bison Range partnering efforts, "if the Salish and Kootenai can reach an agreement with the Fish and Wildlife Service, something will not have been taken from the public. Something will have been added to it." (see copy of editorial below).

The National Bison Range

Later this week Native Americans representing the Salish and Kootenai tribes will meet in Denver with officials of the Interior Department and the federal Fish and Wildlife Service. They will be trying to negotiate an agreement to take over management of the National Bison Range, an 18,500-acre prairie reserve in northwestern Montana. If negotiations end successfully, this would be the first time a tribe has taken over the management of such a property since 1994, when the Tribal Self-Governance Act authorized such arrangements.

One purpose of the Tribal Self-Governance Act was to diminish the role of federal paternalism — often inefficient and sometimes corrupt — in the lives of Native Americans. The Confederated Salish and Kootenai Tribes have been among the first to seize the opportunity to run programs that were formerly administered by the government, and run them well. But the thought of Native Americans' managing the National Bison Range has some environmental groups and local residents worried. Even the Fish and Wildlife Service has seemed reluctant, if only because it has a high regard for its own management tradition. Yet virtually no one disputes the excellent management and conservation record of the Salish and Kootenai.

With one strong condition, we think this plan makes a lot of sense. The Salish and Kootenai have a deep historical connection with the particular bison herd on this refuge — quite apart from the conventional associations of Indians and buffalo — and a strong cultural or historical link is one of the legal conditions for enacting an agreement of this kind, which would basically employ the tribes to manage the federal program. The National Bison Range is wholly enclosed by the reservation the Salish and Kootenai live on, and the tribes would be obliged to manage the refuge according to plans established by the Fish and Wildlife Service.

But such an agreement, erected on the basis of unique historical and geographical circumstances, must not become the basis for the wholesale privatization of federal parks, monuments or reserves. The National Bison Range is an unusual case. It offers a rare convergence of public and tribal interests. If the Salish and Kootenai can reach an agreement with the Fish and Wildlife Service, something will not have been taken from the public. Something will have been added to it.

To this end, I would like to extend the CSKT Tribal Council's sincere appreciation for our friends in Congress who have long supported a Self-Governance partnership at the NBRC.

Provisions of S. 919

As mentioned at the outset of this testimony, CSKT supports S. 919, including the proposed revision currently under the Committee's consideration. Making Titles IV and V of ISDEAA (Interior Self-Governance and Indian Health Service Self-Governance, respectively) more consistent has long been a goal for Self-Governance tribes. CSKT agrees with S. 919's approach of leaving intact much of the existing statute, while amending some of the current provisions and adding new ones.

CSKT greatly appreciates the inclusion in S. 919 of specific recognition that 50 percent of costs incurred by a tribe's governing body are reasonable and allowable for purposes of contract support cost determinations. Including this provision in the statute would bring an end to past uncertainties as to whether the federal government would continue this past practice. This has a significant impact on the budget of CSKT and many other tribes. [§ 104 of S. 919, as introduced]

CSKT particularly supports S. 919's definition for the term "inherent Federal function". While the term is already so defined in Title V, having the definition specifically included for Interior programs is a positive step towards eliminating the confusion over this term during field-level negotiations. [§ 201(a)("401(6)") of S. 919, as introduced]

As the only tribe currently with a Self-Governance agreement with the OST, we also support S. 919's explicit incorporation of the OST with respect to mandatory Self-Governance agreements. [§ 201(c)(1)("(a)(2)")]

CSKT appreciates S. 919's inclusion of specific authority for multi-year funding agreements, as this is an issue for which we have encountered some resistance from federal agencies in the past. We have been able to resolve the disagreements successfully, but statutory clarification will prevent needless disagreements on the issue in the future. [§ 201(c)(1)("(p)(4)")]

CSKT strongly supports the statutory clarification of tribal ability to carry-over funding. This is also an area in which we have had disagreements with federal agencies and we welcome the clarification. [§ 201(d)("408(k)")]

With respect to contract support funding, it is important that S. 919 retains the existing statutory language mandating funding for contract support costs (25 U.S.C. § 458cc(g)(3)). Payment of contract support costs is a prerequisite for realizing the full potential of Tribal Self-Governance objectives. Stronger efforts to secure adequate appropriations for this area are badly needed. In our testimony on prior versions of this legislation, CSKT has repeatedly raised this issue. We have consistently maintained that Congress did not intend for Self-Determination or Self-Governance contracting to be money-losing propositions, yet that is what they have become as long as the federal government refuses to pay tribes what they are due under the law for administration of the programs. Since our last testimony regarding this legislation, the Supreme Court has confirmed, in its *Salazar v. Ramah Navajo Chapter* opinion,[5] that the Federal Government is legally obligated to fully pay these costs. We were very disappointed in the Obama Administration's effort to cap contract support cost payments for fiscal year 2014, thereby preventing tribes from pursuing legal claims for full payment. CSKT very much appreciates Congress' rejection of that approach in the FY14 budget, and we appreciate the leadership of a number of Senators on this Committee in advocating for tribes on this issue.

CSKT supports S. 919's approach of maintaining the existing statutory authority for contracting Interior programs, outside of the BIA, that are of geographic, historical or cultural significance to tribes. It is through the lens of our experiences involving the NBRC that we evaluate the non-BIA provisions of S. 919. The legislation would leave untouched the statutory authority for NBRC contracting, found at 25 U.S.C. § 458cc(c). CSKT supports this since we have negotiated multiple agreements under this authority and do not want to see it diminished or impaired in any way. Section 202 of S. 919, both as introduced and in the Committee's proposed amended version, further clarifies that nothing in this legislation would modify this aspect of non-BIA contracting authority. CSKT would strongly oppose any changes or amendments to non-BIA contracting authority that could be used by opponents of tribal contracting to further hamper or prevent Self-Governance partnerships such as those we have built at the NBRC.

CSKT believes more should be done to encourage, rather than discourage, these partnerships. The United States is rapidly falling far behind countries such as Canada and Australia when it comes to federal-tribal partnerships in the management of protected areas such as refuges and parks. CSKT believes that Tribal Self-Governance policies and agreements have been, and can be, strong vehicles for constructive collaboration between the United States and Indian tribes.

Two areas of continuing concern for CSKT which S. 919 does not currently address include the following:

Federal Tort Claims Act (FTCA) coverage. Presently, liability coverage for tribal contractors, including FTCA coverage, is addressed in Title I of ISDEAA at 25 U.S.C. § 450f(c). In past AFA negotiations, CSKT has expended a disproportionate amount of time and energy over the issue of whether FTCA coverage existed for tribal volunteers who perform work for a contracted federal program. CSKT has long maintained that tribal volunteers performing federal program work should enjoy the same FTCA coverage as federal volunteers performing such work. Unfortunately, we have not resolved this issue and, as a result, the BIA has agreed to purchase liability insurance to cover Tribal volunteers under our last two NBRC AFA's. While we have found agreement with our position from Interior solicitor offices, we understand that opposition emanates from the U.S. Department of Justice (DOJ). We are generally concerned with what seems to be an increasing practice by the DOJ to narrowly interpret FTCA coverage in circumstances involving tribal contractors, as well as in other situations. This unfortunately has had negative impacts on CSKT's ability to recruit volunteers for contracted programs and/or explain to existing or prospective volunteers the scope of their liability coverage. In plain terms, we believe we have lost potential, and past, volunteers at the NBRC due to this issue. We encourage Committee attention to this ongoing problem.

Full funding of programs. CSKT has been on record with equating the issue of full program funding to effective implementation of ISDEAA and Tribal Self-Governance objectives. Without Congressional commitment to fully funding the federal programs being contracted by Self-Governance tribes, we cannot overcome the resource limitations to making the programs as successful as they need to be. Dwindling, or stagnant, federal funding results in tribes having to supplement federal programs with tribal dollars. This serves as a disincentive

---

[5] 132 S.Ct. 2181 (2012).

to contract under ISDEAA and Tribal Self-Governance. Just a couple of the many examples relevant to Title IV contracts include:

• The recently completed third independent assessment and report on the status of Indian forests and forestry finds that BIA funding for Indian trust forest management is $2.82 per acre—an amount which is only one-third of the funding level for the U.S. Forest Service, which is $8.57 per acre.

• Per capita spending on law enforcement in Native American communities is roughly 60 percent of the national average.

Similar disparities exist for almost all Indian programs contracted under Title IV. While this is an appropriations issue and somewhat of a separate issue from the Self-Governance provisions of S. 919, it is materially related to achieving the goals of the Act and is thus a proper subject for this Committee's attention. Congressional rectification of this issue would be a solid investment into more effective program delivery and better administration of the federal trust responsibility.

Conclusion

The Confederated Salish and Kootenai Tribes are one of many tribes that successfully partner with the federal government under the Tribal Self-Governance rubric. Work remains to be done towards: (1) eliminating disincentives and removing barriers to Self-Governance participation; and (2) encouraging non-BIA Self-Governance activity. The proposed legislation is a good start towards accomplishing those ends.

On behalf of CSKT, thank you for the opportunity to provide testimony and I would like to thank this Committee, its Members, and staff, for your support of Self-Governance. I would be happy to answer any questions.

Attachments

Jeff King,
Refuge Manager,
National Bison Range,
Moiese, MT 59824

RE: SCOPING COMMENTS—NOTICE OF INTENT TO PREPARE AN ENVIRONMENTAL ASSESSMENT REGARDING THE INTEREST OF THE CONFEDERATED SALISH AND KOOTENAI TRIBES TO ENTER INTO AN ANNUAL FUNDING AGREEMENT WITH THE U. S. FISH AND WILDLIFE SERVICE (''THE SERVICE''), FOR THE OPERATION AND MANAGEMENT OF PROGRAMS AT THE NATIONAL BISON RANGE COMPLEX

Dear Mr. King,

Thank you for the opportunity to provide comments concerning your notice of intent to prepare an Environmental Assessment regarding the Annual Funding Agreement (AFA) with Confederated Salish and Kootenai Tribes (CSKT) and the National Bison Range (NBR). The National Wildlife Federation (NWF) is America's largest conservation organization and has over 4 million supporters and 47 state affiliates. NWF has a long history of partnering with Native American Tribes to conserve and protect wildlife for our children's future and currently partners with the CSKT on numerous wildlife, habitat and environmental issues.

NWF strongly believes that a partnership between the Service and the CSKT should be formalized through a new self-governance AFA that would contract with the CSKT to operate eligible refuge programs and perform specific day-to-day activities of the NBR consistent with the National Wildlife Refuge System Administration Act (NWRSAA). NWF has supported this partnership since it was originally proposed in 2004.

On May 17, 2012, the CSKT's received NWF's National Government Conservation Achievement Awards for their outstanding commitment to preserving, protecting and restoring wildlife and habitat for future generations. [1] The CSKT is unparalleled in their methods, efforts, conservation ethic and follow through to achieve sustainable conservation outcomes. Known throughout the country for their scientific and cultural knowledge, their partnerships with other governments and long history of conserving, managing and restoring wildlife habitat, the CSKT Division of Fish, Wildlife, Conservation and Recreation are more than qualified to partner with the Service to manage NBR's resources.

As you know, the CSKT's have a long history of managing wildlife and wild lands in partnership with local, state and Federal governments. For example, they have,

---

[1] Missoulian, *http://missoulian.com/news/state-and-regional/salish-kootenai-tribes-win-national-conservation-award/article*10e02a208–9fc2–11e1–9d9d-0019bb2963f4.html.

- Signed a historic landmark agreement in 1990 between the Tribes and the state of Montana governing bird hunting and fishing on the Flathead Indian Reservation.
- Successfully managed 97,000 acres of primitive areas.
- Acquired and managed over 11,000 acres of fish and wildlife habitat through the Tribal Wildlife Management Program.
- Acquired over 4,600 acres of land, including 27 miles of streams and lake habitat to offset impacts to fisheries.

The National Bison Range is an outstanding and important resource for all Americans and the CSKT are outstanding land and wildlife managers that preserve and protect wildlife in one of the most important ecosystems in North America. The Tribes helped save the bison in the 19th and early 20th centuries and will continue to protect the bison and other wildlife species and natural resources on the NBR for future generations.

We believe that this partnership will produce numerous long-term benefits to the Tribes, the Service and all Americans. The agreement will utilize the best abilities and resources of the Tribes and the Federal Government to manage NBR's resources and better serve the people that utilize the land. This partnership will also facilitate the achievement of Departmental and Congressional objectives for both its NWRS and Tribal Self-Governance programs. The Tribe is in a strong legal position to participate in the AFA. The Tribal Self-Governance Act of 1994 gives qualified Indian tribes the right to request funding agreements to perform activities administered by the Department of Interior that are of special geographic, historic or cultural significance to the requesting tribe. It is well known that the NBR has a very high level of cultural, historic and geographic significance to the CSKT and all units of the NBR under consideration for an AFA are located within the Flathead Reservation. Many of the bison that reside on the NBR are descendants from a herd originally saved by Tribal members in the late 19th century, and which originated on the reservation.

We look forward to working with the Service and CSKT on the Environmental Assessment for the AFA.

Sincerely,

31

LARRY SCHWEIGER, PRESIDENT AND CEO,
National Wildlife Federation.

Honorable Dirk Kempthorne
Secretary
Department of the Interior
1849 C Street, NW
Washington, DC 20240

Dear Mr. Secretary,

As Chairman and Ranking Member of the Committee with jurisdiction over Indian legislation and the National Wildlife Refuge System, we wish to convey our support for the proposal by the Confederated Salish and Kootenai Tribes (CSKT) of the Flathead Reservation to manage and operate the National Bison Range Complex (NBRC) via an Annual Funding Agreement (AFA) with the U.S. Fish & Wildlife Service (FWS) under the Tribal Self-Governance Act. We also are concerned that the lack of support of this agreement by some individuals within the FWS may have resulted in a distorted record concerning NBR activities under the AFA.

The Indian Self-Determination Act and the Tribal Self-Governance Act allow qualified tribes to contract to perform the activities of the Federal government for local program management. As part of the Tribal Self-Governance Act (Act), Congress specifically authorized tribes to manage certain types of non-Bureau of Indian Affairs programs within the Department of the Interior (Department). The Committee Report accompanying the Act (H. Rpt. 103-653) makes it clear that the Act applies to FWS programs and, in particular, to circumstances such as those found at the NBRC. We specifically stated in the Committee Report: *The Committee intends this provision in conjunction with the rest of the Act, to ensure that any federal activity carried out by the Secretary within the exterior boundaries of the reservation shall be presumptively eligible for inclusion in the Self-Governance funding agreement.* As you know, the entire National Bison Range, along with its ancillary Ninepipe and Pablo Refuges, are located within the exterior boundaries of the Flathead Indian Reservation.

CSKT's connections to the NBRC, and its bison, make for unique circumstances. Also in this instance, CSKT owns the land on which two of the NBRC's ancillary refuges are located. In fact, the Ninepipe and Pablo National Wildlife Refuges are operated by FWS pursuant to easements obtained from CSKT. Another compelling fact is that the bison at the NRBC consist of descendants of a bison herd that was owned by CSKT Tribal members over a century ago. That herd was started and managed by Tribal members at a time when the bison were on the verge of extinction due to non-Indian activities.

Under the Act, the Department is required to publish annually a list of non-BIA Interior programs that are eligible for compacting under Self-Governance. Currently, of the 546 refuges that exist in this country, the FWS list identifies only 18 in the lower 48 states and 16 in Alaska as eligible. Three of the 18 are wholly located within the Flathead Indian Reservation and are part of the NBRC. Since enactment of the Act, 13 years ago, there have been only two AFAs with the FWS: the first involving the Council of Athabascan Tribal Governments exclusively for project work at the Yukon Flats National Wildlife Refuge in Alaska; and the second being the CSKT-FWS AFA for the NBRC. In short, a very small percent of the Refuge System is listed as even being eligible for contracting, and of those 34 refuges, only two have tribal contracts associated with them.

The National Wildlife Refuge Administration Act (the Administration Act) does not prohibit the delegation of management activities to non-federal entities. To the contrary, the Administration Act makes multiple references to working with State governments on refuge programs: mandates that the Interior Secretary ensure coordination, interaction, and cooperation with adjacent landowners and State fish and wildlife agencies; requires the Interior Secretary to cooperate and collaborate with Federal agencies and State fish and wildlife agencies when managing refuges; and specifically authorizes FWS to "enter into cooperative agreements with State fish and wildlife agencies for the management of programs on a refuge." (16 U.S.C. § 668dd (b)(4)) (emphasis added). Working with Tribal governments in the same manner under the authorization of the Tribal Self-Governance Act should not be viewed any differently than partnering with State governments especially in this instance where the tribe owns the land on which the ancillary facilities of the NBRC National Bison Range Complex are located.

Some critics of the AFA have said that the principle of the 1976 amendments to the Administration Act was that there should never be any attempt to establish a second National Wildlife Refuge System by delegating FWS authorities to non-federal entities. We do not believe allowing CSKT to help manage the NBRC is creating a second refuge system. To the contrary, we see it as a logical partnership under both the Administration Act and the Tribal Self-Governance Act. Although the Refuge System's organic Act was significantly amended by the 1997 National Wildlife Refuge System Improvement Act, this law did not prohibit Tribal Self-Governance agreements.

This type of partnership is even encouraged by Executive Order 12996, entitled "Management and General Public Use of the National Wildlife Refuge System." Section 2(c) says:

"Partnerships. America's sportsmen and women were the first partners who insisted on protecting valuable wildlife habitat within wildlife refuges. Conservation partnerships with other Federal agencies, State agencies, Tribes, organizations, industry, and the general public can make significant contributions to the growth and management of the Refuge System."

As we are both strong supporters of the Refuge System, we would be concerned if the NBRC AFA could serve as a precursor to privatization of refuges. Yet we are convinced that this is not the case. Agreements with other governments — be they State or Tribal — are not comparable to privatization schemes where for-profit entities take over federal programs. A Tribal government is not a corporate entity any more than a federal, state or local government is a corporate entity. Under the AFA and the Tribal Self-Governance Act, the NBRC remains a federally-owned Refuge and all applicable federal statutes and regulations that apply to the Refuge System continue to apply under the AFA. In the absence of compliance with this requirement, we would not support the NBRC AFA.

The CKST have demonstrated a high level of performance in contracting a wide variety of other federal programs. Under their AFA, CSKT has stated repeatedly its commitment to operate the NBRC pursuant to the laws and regulations applicable to all refuges. In fact, the Act contains safeguards that protect against any jeopardy to natural resources or other federal assets. We understand that CSKT is the first tribe to designate an official wilderness: the Mission Mountain Tribal Wilderness Area. Their efforts have led to that area being one the few places in Montana where there are grizzly bears. The CSKT also manage a large herd of Bighorn sheep, and they worked with the FWS to reintroduce the Trumpeter Swan to the Flathead Valley. In short, CSKT has excellent credentials to manage wildlife-related programs at the NBRC.

We also understand that, beyond the scope of work required of it through the AFA, the CSKT has devoted extensive tribal resources to the NBRC. At a time when the overall National Wildlife Refuge System budget has suffered, CSKT employees and volunteers literally worked thousands of hours at the NBRC. If a new AFA, with broader tribal management, might result in a continuation of that degree of tribal supplementation at a federal refuge, we would think the Department would do everything in its power to make it happen.

Finally, we are concerned to hear of the recent development wherein the FWS is proposing to radically downsize the number of staff and bison at the NBRC. The proposed reduction from 20 full time staff down to 6 staff is no way for the FWS to treat the refuge it recently referred to as the Refuge System's "Crown Jewel" nor does it make sense to reduce the number of bison from over 300 animals down to 100. Such cuts are not merely the NBRC's proportionate share of agency wide reductions, rather, they have every appearance of being proposals intended to make the CSKT disinterested in future management of the NBRC. We hope you will immediately reverse these proposed reductions.

We hope you agree that promoting a fair implementation of a Tribal Self-Governance AFA at the National Bison Range furthers important congressional and federal objectives as identified in both the Administration Act and the Tribal Self-Governance Act.

Sincerely,

NICK J. RAHALL, II
Chairman

DON YOUNG
Ranking Member

The CHAIRWOMAN. Thank you, Mr. Trahan. Again, thanks for that invitation. You do represent a beautiful part of our Country, so you never know when some of us might show up.

We are going to wait on questions, we are going to go to Mr. Isaac next, and when we have finished with him and Mr. Peercy, then we will go to questions. Thank you for your testimony.

Mr. Isaac?

STATEMENT OF JERRY ISAAC, PRESIDENT, TANANA CHIEFS CONFERENCE

Mr. ISAAC. Thank you, Chairwoman Cantwell, Vice Chairman Barrasso and the rest of the Committee, Senator Murkowski and Senator Tester.

Thank you so much for holding today's hearing on S. 919. I too will read my testimony. As I noted in my written testimony, this is likely my last opportunity to testify before Congress on behalf of Tanana Chiefs Conference. So today is a very special day for me.

Thank you to the Committee for inviting me. But more importantly, thank you for all that you have done to help Indian Country and that you continue to do to help Indian Country.

I have witnessed incredible change in the past decades, all for the good. Much of it is attributable to the work of this Committee. I am here today to support enactment of S. 919, so that the rules for compacting with the Department of the Interior will finally be consistent with the successful compacting rules that control the Indian Health Services.

Title 4 and Title 5 are part of one law, the Indian Self-Determination Act. We deal with two agencies, IHS and BIA. But there is just one law and there should just be one set of rules to follow.

In my written testimony I mentioned on good example of how self-governance suffers when there are two different sets of rules. In the IHS rule, we sometimes have delays with IHS in negotiating a new funding agreement on a new funding table. When that happens, thanks to Title 5, our old funding agreement with IHS remains in place. Funding continues, services continue. The old agreement stays in place until there is a new agreement.

But in the BIA world, a negotiation delay means funding stops, services stop, the compacting relationship essentially stops. This is not just a timing issue. Because of these different rules Interior can and in the past Interior has refused to sign a new agreement unless we accept Interior's demands for unilateral changes in those agreements or in the funding tables. That kind of pressure tactic is unacceptable. It is contrary to the core principle of tribal self-governance and the whole idea of government to government relations.

I am pleased to say that the current Administration has not pressured tribes in this fashion. The new bill will make certain that these improvements and current practice will become improvements in the law. But no contracting law alone can address our most severe problems. Those include the terrible abuse suffered by women in some of our villages. The recent Law and Order Commission report once again put a spotlight on this terrible issue and on the barriers that are preventing our local tribal governments from doing more to help.

I am extremely pleased to see that Senator Murkowski and Senator Begich have committed in S. 1474 to repeal Section 910 of the Violence Against Women Act. All I would ask is that the Committee consider adding that one provision into this bill. Our women are suffering and our tribes lack the tools they need to do something about it. They cannot wait, our women cannot wait.

So I hope that this is something the Committee can consider adding to S. 919 as this important bill moves forward. It all relates to improving the ability of our tribes to maximize tribal self-governance and make the communities safe and healthier for all.

Before closing, I want to offer a special thanks to the Committee for being such a champion on the contract support cost issue. Thanks in major part to your two hearings, the 2014 Omnibus Appropriation rejected efforts to convert our self-governance compacts into little more than discretionary grants. I thank you.

But more work remains to be done. All of the past contract support cost claims need to finally be resolved. We have waited too long, 20 years. This makes no sense. Not when the agencies have already told Congress how much they owe. I am confident that with your continuing support, these claims can at long last be concluded.

Thank you for the privilege of appearing today. Thanks to the Indian self-Determination act, our villages are stronger and our futures are brighter. Most importantly, our vision remains unchanged for all tribes, including Alaska tribes, to be vested with the power and resources necessary to assure safe, healthy and sustainable communities. I thank you again.

[The prepared statement of Mr. Isaac follows:]

PREPARED STATEMENT OF JERRY ISAAC, PRESIDENT, TANANA CHIEFS CONFERENCE

Chairwoman Cantwell, Vice-Chairman Barrasso and distinguished Members of the Committee, thank you so much for holding today's hearing on S. 919, a bill that would finally conform the rules for compacting with the Department of the Interior, to the rules which have long controlled tribal compacting with the Department of Health and Human Services.

My name is Jerry Isaac, and I am the President of the Tanana Chiefs Conference. TCC is an intertribal consortium of 37 federally recognized Tribes located in the Interior of Alaska. We serve approximately 13,000 tribal members in our villages and in Fairbanks. Our traditional territory occupies a largely road less area that is almost the size of Texas, stretching from Fairbanks clear up to the Brooks Range, and over to the Canadian border.

TCC was one of the first tribal organizations to move from self-determination contracting to self-governance compacting. We made this move shortly after passage of the 1988 Tribal Self-Governance Demonstration Project Act, and we continued after the demonstration program became permanent with the 1994 enactment of Title IV.

TCC is unique in its relationship with its Member Tribes. This is because, as an inter-tribal organization, our mission is to do everything possible to facilitate maximum local self-governance by the Tribes. To carry out that mission, we have extensive inter-tribal agreements with each of our Member Tribes so that each Village develops the right mix of locally and regionally administered programs. As a result of our local empowerment strategies, our Member Tribes have substantially enhanced their self-governing capabilities in a wide range of areas including tribal courts, child welfare and family services, housing, welfare assistance, roads, and education. The flexibility provided by the self-governance rules has been a vital part of that success.

There is no question in anyone's mind that tribal self-governance works, and for this reason TCC strongly supports prompt enactment of S. 919. This legislation is needed because the controlling legislation (Title IV) has failed to keep up with the times, so that today we operate under two very different self-governance regimes: one for the Interior Department, and the other (Title V) with the Department of Health and Human Services. This makes no sense, and at times it has created an administrative and legal nightmare for TCC.

Let me offer just one example. When there are negotiation delays in the execution of a new funding agreement with IHS, our old funding agreement with IHS remains in place and the funding continues to flow. Services continue uninterrupted. But with Interior, the absence of an executed new funding agreement means everything stops. This is not just a timing issue: because of these different rules, Interior can—and in the past Interior has—<u>refused</u> to sign a new agreement and refused to release funding unless we first accepted Interior's demands for unilateral changes in our agreements—or even mid-term changes in footnotes to the so-called "reprogramming" requests. This kind of pressure tactic is contrary to the policy of self-governance and has long been eliminated in the IHS self-governance world. While the current Administration has not pressured Tribes in this fashion, the new bill makes certain these on-the-ground improvements will be permanent and a matter of law.

We applaud the work of the Committee's staff, the Department's lawyers, and the tribal drafting team for working so hard over so many years to develop an amended bill that is acceptable to everyone. It is an important compromise where each side has had to give a little to achieve an acceptable whole. For TCC, we believe the time is long past to promptly move the bill through mark-up and final passage.

Before closing I do need to pause and note a critical related issue, because it impacts the funding that comes to TCC under its self-governance compact. As things stand today, Alaska tribes and tribal consortiums are unable to access BIA tribal courts funding. While this has been a problem before, the absence of that funding has been worsened by recently-enacted section 910 of the Violence Against Women Act. Section 910 now blocks our villages from taking critical steps to protect Native women, and it takes away a major tool that our villages had used to protect vulnerable and battered women. It is imperative that Congress promptly repeal section 910, and if that is possible in this bill, TCC would urge that it be done.

Finally, I note that the one area where self-governance has faltered is in the area of contract support costs. This Committee has been a true champion for Tribes on this issue and held, not one, but <u>two</u>, hearings on this issue last year. We salute the Committee and the very positive outcome reflected in the FY 2014 Omnibus appropriation. Now what remains is to facilitate the resolution of past claims, so that we can turn the page on this unfortunate chapter in our march forward to greater tribal self-determination and self-governance.

This is likely my last opportunity to testify before Congress as President of TCC, since my term concludes in a few weeks. It has been a privilege and a true honor to represent our Tribes, and to work with this remarkable Committee to protect and enhance the interests of all Native American Tribes. I have witnessed incredible change in the past decades, all for the good. Our villages are stronger, our futures are brighter, and our vision remains unchanged for Tribes in Alaska to be vested with the full power and resources necessary to assure safe, healthy and sustainable communities.

The CHAIRWOMAN. Thank you.
Mr. Peercy, welcome. Thank you for being here.

STATEMENT OF MICKEY PEERCY, EXECUTIVE DIRECTOR OF SELF–GOVERNANCE, CHOCTAW NATION OF OKLAHOMA

Mr. PEERCY. Thank you, Senator. I will read some of mine then I will talk some of mine. I talk better than I read. I would ask Chairman Allen to catch me if I get out of line. They say I don't have a filter, but I know I do.

The CHAIRWOMAN. You have a clock, for sure.

Mr. PEERCY. I have a clock, and it is running.

[Laughter.]

Mr. PEERCY. That is what I get I ramble.

On behalf of Chief Gregory Pyle and the Council at Choctaw Nation, I want to thank you for all your support of this distinguished Committee and also for your action on S. 919 as well as the 11 cosponsors.

Choctaw Nation began in this self-governance journey in 1994, 1995, respectively, with IHS and the Bureau of Indian Affairs. It is the Chief's and Council's responsibility to always look after their people and also to do everything possible to guarantee self-sufficiency of the people and the Nation.

BIA, the Chief would not have me come here if I didn't say that means bossing Indians around. He is confidently saying that. And it is an issue. Go with me just a little bit to Ardmore, Oklahoma and an Indian family that has an IM account, they have issues with money. Refrigerator goes out, so they load up the children, they load up the family and they drive up to the agency's office and they go ask the social worker first, then they ask the superintendent of the agency if they can have enough money to buy a refrigerator. It is not right. There is nothing right about that in terms of the dignity of the Indian family, of any family of anyone. It is not acceptable.

The tribe does everything that it can to build self-sufficiency within self-governance, to build the self-sufficiency of the family as well as the Nation. So those sorts of indignities don't happen. S. 919 makes it a high priority of self-governance tribes in our quest to get legislation enacted that will remove many of the administrative and practical barriers that persist and have persisted in Title 4.

The current law, as it is, allows for delays and obstruction by the DOI which has resulted in frustration for tribes through self-governance implementation process. Instead of operating program services, functions and activities in an efficient and productive manner as originally intended, and performed under the self-governance demonstration projects, tribes have been subject to pushbacks constantly in the system. This cannot work any longer.

In testimony with Dr. Roubideaux at one time, four or five years ago, I wrote in written testimony as well as speaking that the Indian Health Service, we were talking about contract health service. I had made the statement that the Indian Health Service didn't have the DNA to do contract health service. It wasn't personal. It is the fact that the management of that program, they weren't able to do it, they weren't able to get doctors paid on time and they didn't seem to have the willingness to do what it took. Dr. Roubideaux still hasn't forgiven me for that.

But it is the case here. It is the case when we have Federal people, and I appreciate this Committee and I appreciate Kevin Washburn, he is Chickasaw, they live right next door to us, and I appreciate the political people, all the secretaries, all the heads that are political, I don't care if it is Republican or Democrat, they can't do it. It is the career people who stop the progress.

And I will say that, I am probably going to retire in about four or five years, but I am going to say that going to my grave, that there is an inherent thing going on, and I have seen two decades of Federal people. So it is not just one decade, it is the next decade. I have been doing this since 1985. And there is an inherent need to be paternalistic, especially with the Bureau. And until laws are set and regulations are set that challenges that and makes it easier to go down that road, we are going to be stuck where we are.

With that, I know I am a little bit over, about five seconds. We are humble but proud, we are strong and will continue to grow and succeed. But most of all, we believe that we made the right choice putting our tribe under self-governance. We need new tools, we need new tools to make sure that we are refining the process, building upon the initiative and government-to-government relationships so that we can successfully continue this point. S. 919 is one of those tools.

Thank you for your patience. We are here to answer any of those hard questions.

[The prepared statement of Mr. Peercy follows:]

PREPARED STATEMENT OF MICKEY PEERCY, EXECUTIVE DIRECTOR OF SELF-GOVERNANCE, CHOCTAW NATION OF OKLAHOMA

On behalf of Chief Gregory Pyle and the Choctaw Nation of Oklahoma, thank you Vice-Chairman Barrasso for inviting Choctaw to testify and thank you to the Senate Committee on Indian Affairs for convening this hearing on S. 919. We would also like to thank the eleven co-sponsors who by their very actions represent the continued belief in Congress that Self-Governance works!

The Choctaw Nation of Oklahoma is an American Indian Tribe organized pursuant to the provisions of the Indian Reorganization Act of June 26, 1936–49. Stat. 1967. and is Federally recognized by the United States Government through the Secretary of the Interior. The Choctaw Nation of Oklahoma consists of ten and one-half counties in the southeastern part of Oklahoma and is bordered on the east by the State of Arkansas, on the south by the Red River, on the north by the South Canadian, Canadian and Arkansas Rivers, and on the west by a line slightly west of Durant that runs north to the South Canadian River.

We have been operating under a compact of Self-Governance since 1995 in the Indian Health Service/Department of Health and Human Service and since 1996 in the Bureau of Indian Affairs/Department of the Interior. The Choctaw Nation of Oklahoma believes that responsibility for achieving self-sufficiency rests with the governing body of the Tribe. It is the Tribal Council's responsibility to assist our community in its ability to implement an economic development strategy and to plan, organize and direct Tribal resources in a comprehensive manner which results in self-sufficiency. The Tribal Council recognizes the need to strengthen the Nation's economy, with primary efforts being focused on the creation of additional job opportunities through promotion and development. By planning and developing its own programs and building a strong economic base, the Choctaw Nation of Oklahoma applies its own fiscal, natural, and human resources to develop self-sufficiency. These efforts can only succeed through strong governance, sound economic development and positive social development.

S. 919 remains a top priority for Self-Governance Tribes in our quest to get legislation enacted that will remove many of the administrative and impractical barriers that have persisted with Title IV since 1994. For more than a decade, we have developed and refined proposed amendments to Title IV of the Indian Self-Determination and Education Assistance Act (P.L. 93–638, as amended). These amendments would achieve consistency between Titles IV and V of the Act and address problems which affect the ability of Self-Governance Tribes to better serve our citizens. The Choctaw Nation, along with other Self-Governance Tribal leaders, have worked tirelessly with the Administration and Congress on these amendments. We strongly believe it is time to move forward with enactment and we urge this Committee to support and advance S. 919.

Since we began this effort, many Tribal leaders have testified before the Senate Committee on Indian Affairs (SCIA) regarding on-going problems implementing Self-Governance in DOI. These problems, ranging from inadequate funding levels to bureaucratic recalcitrance, have caused increased participation by new Tribes in

Tribal Self-Governance to lessen considerably; which is unfortunate since Self-Governance has proven to dramatically improve the efficiency, accountability and effectiveness of programs and services for many Tribes and their citizens.

The current law allows for delays and obstruction by the DOI which has resulted in frustration for Tribes throughout the Self-Governance implementation process. Instead of operating programs, services, functions and activities in an efficient and productive manner as originally intended and performed under the Self-Governance Demonstration Project, Tribes have been subjected to "push back" and recalcitrance from the DOI to fully implement the full spirit of the Act. This was spearheaded by the 1996 Title IV negotiated rulemaking process which failed and left the Tribes with a sense of urgency to remedy the ills that were created by the promulgation of the rules and contrary to the sense of Congress in enacting the legislation.

All but a very few S. 919 provisions were negotiated and agreed to by Tribal and Federal representatives. The vast majority of the proposed amendments are not new or radical ideas—many have been adapted from the Department of Health and Human Services (DHHS) version of Self-Governance, codified as Title V of the Indian Self-Determination and Education Assistance Act of 1975 (ISDEAA).

In 2000, Congress enacted Title V which permanently authorized Self-Governance in the Indian Health Service (IHS), within DHHS. Many of the improvements and Tribal authority reflected in Title V remain absent from Title IV Bureau of Indian Affairs (BIA) program administration. Consequently, many Self-Governance Tribes are forced to operate under two separate administrative requirements, one for IHS and one for BIA. The proposed bill will bring Title IV into line with Title V.

The lack of administrative efficiencies under Title IV—has been costly for Tribes in terms of time, money and loss of opportunities to strengthen Tribal infrastructures and develop competitive reservation economies. The IHS Title V amendments provide for the timely distribution of funding and administrative safeguards for Tribes aligning the implementation of executive branch regulatory authority with the congressional intent of the ISDEAA. Like the Title V amendments, S. 919 intends to clarify and expand the provisions of ISDEAA and streamline efficiencies and administrative provisions of the Act.

There have been many studies and reports performed to evaluate BIA management, organizational structure and administration, as well as to identify and recommend remedies to improve quality, efficiency and cost-effectiveness, organization, functionality and performance.

The 1999 National Academy of Public Administrators (NAPA) Report,[1] stated ". . . without major management and organizational reforms, the BIA will be unable both to fully meet its responsibilities to the 1.4 million American Indians and Alaska Natives it serves and to operate an effective and efficient agency. BIA does not have the capacity to effectively perform basic Federal functions of accounting, property management, human resources management, procurement, and information resources management. Further complicating matters at the BIA is the fact that staff do not receive adequate training." The implementation of the recommendations in the NAPA Report commenced in 2004.

In 2011, the Bronner Group[2] was engaged to perform a multi-phase evaluation relating to the administrative support structure of the BIA which included evaluating the NAPA Report. For purposes of the Bronner Report, the term "support functions" included accounting/finance, budget, acquisitions/contracting, property management, safety management, human resources, information technology, as well as engineering and facilities management. In March 2012 the Bronner Report was released and the reorganization of Indian Affairs was launched much to the chagrin of the Tribes.

In February 2013 the Government Accountability Office prepared a study on *Management Challenges Continue to Hinder Efforts to Improve Indian Education*[3] which identified challenges within the Department of the Interior's Office of the Assistant Secretary—Indian Affairs (IA), such as fragmented administrative structures and frequent turnover in leadership.

I reference these reports to emphasize the critical need for streamlining the administrative process for Self-Governance Tribes as identified in S. 919 that will allow Self-Governance Tribes to maximize their capability to efficiently and effectively implement Self-Governance at the reservation level. It is unfair to expect that excellence can be achieved by the Tribes when there is such a lack of administrative, program and operational structure in DOI. Removing these barriers will allow

---

[1] National Academy of Public Administrators Report, *Study of Management and Administration*, 1999.
[2] Bronner Report, *A New Day for Indian Affairs*, March 2012.
[3] GAO–13–342T, February 27, 3013.

Self-Governance Tribes the opportunity to succeed where the government is failing them.

Our experience in Self-Governance has allowed us to determine the best mechanisms for delivering financial resources and decisionmaking on our homelands. We were provided the funding to begin to plan for another type of reform to Self-Determination contracting and we have proven that we made a wise choice with Self-Governance. We made substantial progress under the Demonstration Project and we continue to advance our Tribally-driven initiative to quantum leaps today. In DOI, Self-Goverance has grown to include 260 Federally-recognized Tribes; and, in IHS there are 340 Self-Governance Tribes.

We are humble but proud; we are strong and will continue to grow and succeed; but most of all, we believe that we made the right choice for our Tribe under Self-Governance. We need new tools to make sure we are refining the process, building upon the initiative and the government-to-government relationship so that we can successfully continue along this path.

Today, S. 919 is that tool!

Thank you.

The CHAIRWOMAN. Thank you. Again, I appreciate all of you being here and your testimony. My own personal beliefs are that we live in a flat world. That just means with technology and information, you have to drive it down to the level of expertise where people see what the problems are, and empower them to deal with them. The more hierarchical you are, the more you are going to hold people back.

So to me, self-governance makes total sense, and the progress that has been made by self-governing tribes, as I mentioned earlier, Alaska Native Medical Center is a great example of a shining institution that has dealt with a lot of health care problems very adequately, juxtaposed to an IHS delivery system, which can be definitely not innovating at the level that they are innovating.

So anyway, I wanted to ask, I am going to start with you, Mr. Isaac. You say the Administration is, one of the questions I have is about the Department of Interior's refusal to enter into agreements unless the tribe agrees to new terms. You said that this Administration has not engaged in that behavior, which I am happy to hear, but I would like to know for the record, what were the Department's justifications for asking for long-time self-governance tribes to agree to new terms before continuing existing programs?

Mr. ISAAC. I would like to have my staff attorney answer that.

The CHAIRWOMAN. Or he can answer that in writing.

Mr. Isaac, I also had a question for you as it relates to the appraisal process. This is one of the things that your self-governance efforts took over that otherwise would have been done by the Office of Trustee, is that correct?

Mr. ISAAC. Beg pardon?

The CHAIRWOMAN. The Tanana Chiefs Conference self-governance compact with the Department included real estate appraisals. So you would, these would otherwise be done by the Special Trustee. So in doing these real estate appraisals, which is a big issue for the Committee in general, it seems that you were able to manage that within your own community and then had some success on that. Is that correct?

Mr. ISAAC. Yes. We were one of the consortia that early on took on the self-governance compacting. And in my opinion self-governance allows tribes to be self-reliant. And it not only stop there with contracting BIA programs that include realty, it also should strongly consider the inclusion of National Park Service, Bureau of Land

41

Management, any and all Department of the Interior bureau responsibilities I think should be subject to contracting by local tribes.

I am confident to say that we have faced extraordinary circumstances that we prevailed upon and that if any contract survived being underfunded with contract support costs, in the past, I am sure that that group of people would be the ones that I would award contracts to.

The CHAIRWOMAN. So do you see how you improved the management of those, because you were doing the appraisals or overseeing the real estate appraisals? Do you think that enabled more results as it related to settlements?

Mr. ISAAC. Yes. When we are dealing with realty issues, we are more successful at it in that we close out cases, pending files and this stuff more rapidly than it had been in the past. Realty is something that carries trust responsibility along with it, and no doubt it is the Federal trust responsibility that is transferred to the consortia, TCC. And we honor that, we do the best we can to be more prompt and more effective in the delivery of that service.

The CHAIRWOMAN. Thank you.

Senator Tester?

Senator TESTER. Thank you, Madam Chair.

I would just say, on the land buyback issue, and I know the Department probably wants to do it, but I really think we can get more bang for the buck contracting that out to the local level, you guys know what the land is worth, you know much more about the landscape if you are Salish living in Montana than somebody back here.

Now if I was going to say, I am not sure I would want the Salish to do the contract for the Oklahoma tribe. But you guys ought to do your own.

Anyway, that is off topic here for a bit, but maybe not.

Mr. Allen, I think that just about everybody on this Committee agrees that self-governance is a positive thing, and it is undeniable that Indian Country has had some difficulty, and reasonably so in certain areas. Could you give me an idea on some areas in which you believed increased systematic support from the Federal Government would make a positive impact?

Mr. ALLEN. Some areas that we have taken over?

Senator TESTER. Or some areas that maybe haven't done so well that additional help from the Federal Government would help.

Mr. ALLEN. I think the best way to respond to that question is that as the tribes take over programs, A, B and C, it could be a natural resources program, law enforcement program, et cetera. So as a general observation, our analysis is that we are severely underfunded categorically. And so what we have been doing over the years is documenting what that underfunding level is. You can take these programs like natural resource management, wouldn't matter whether it was grazing, timber, fisheries, et cetera, you will see that the tribe are taking those, the Federal component, and then more often than not have added our own resources to supplement in order to get it handled correctly.

Senator TESTER. So a little more funding so you wouldn't have to supplement those with others that should be used in some other program?

Mr. ALLEN. Basically, for the most part, tribes are subsidizing Federal functions. Categorically. You can go across every one of them.

Senator TESTER. I appreciate that.

Chairman Trahan, there have been some recent setbacks in negotiations in the annual funding agreement between your tribe and Fish and Wildlife Service over the management of the Bison Range Complex. The work has been done, I think it was a positive step in the right direction. I would like to hear some more on the National Bison Range Complex and how Indian Country can work with the U.S. Government to increase access and appreciation for public lands, such as the National Bison Range.

Mr. TRAHAN. Madam Chair, Senator Tester, I would gladly like to revert that to one of my staff.

Senator TESTER. You can, or you can respond in writing on that. That would be fine, that would be better yet.

In your testimony you talked about, and this is for you again, Chairman Trahan, you met with the Fish and Wildlife Service recently, maybe even today. And you continue to work on negotiating the annual funding agreement. I think everybody on this Committee wants to see that through, I know you guys want to see it through.

Could CSKT be able to provide the Committee with a progress report in early summer, where things stand on the Bison Range agreement?

Mr. TRAHAN. Sure. We would be happy to do that in the early spring to late summer.

Senator TESTER. Whatever is appropriate.

Mr. TRAHAN. And we would like to also see if the service would like to do it jointly.

Senator TESTER. Say that again?

Mr. TRAHAN. I said, we would also like to ask the Service if they would do a joint briefing with us.

Senator TESTER. That would be good.

The Salish Kootenai tribes have some experience with Mission Valley Power. As we talked about earlier, I think the work you have done there is pretty impressive. I think it provides a model of how Indian Country can really work with State and local governments and do it in a way that I think helps everybody.

Could you tell a little bit more about how operating this public utility has affected the tribe's relationship with the surrounding community?

Mr. TRAHAN. We could do that in writing, but I could give you a short version. It has made a lot of difference within the community, because it has brought the communities more, they understand that the tribe is not trying there to hurt them, it is trying to be helpful to everyone. That is what it has done, it has kept the rates low and everything else in that perspective.

So it has kind of got rid of the big scare that everybody thought there was there with tribes managing something like that.

Senator TESTER. And just out of curiosity, how much of that power is used on tribal lands and how much is used off of tribal lands? Do you know that off the top of your head?

Mr. TRAHAN. I sure don't.

Senator TESTER. George, do you know that?

Mr. WATERS. Certainly a larger percentage, Senator, of the users are not Indians on the reservation. As I mentioned earlier, what we think is fascinating is that there are actually more non-Indians that are asking to become part of the project, which I think is a testimonial to how well it has been run.

Senator TESTER. I think it is a testimonial to the success and the management of it.

I want to thank all four of the folks who testified here today. As we think of additional questions, we may ask you for some answers in writing. Thank you all for being here, thank you for your advocacy of self-determination.

The CHAIRWOMAN. I want to thank the witnesses for your testimony today and for all of the input that you have given. You all represent a lot of information as it relates to the history of self-governance and what has been going right. Now we just have to formalize that so we can move more of Indian Country in that direction.

So we thank you for your testimony. We look forward to moving this bill in the near future and seeing if we can get it onto the President's desk after getting it through the House of Representatives.

This hearing is adjourned.

[Whereupon, at 4:02 p.m., the Committee was adjourned.]

APPENDIX

PREPARED STATEMENT OF HON. BRIAN SCHATZ, U.S. SENATOR FROM HAWAII

I want to thank Senators Cantwell and Barrasso for holding this important hearing today to consider, S. 919, the Department of the Interior Tribal Self-Governance Act. Since this may be the last legislative hearing you two chair together, I also want to let the Chair and Vice Chair know how much I appreciate the bipartisan working relationship you have forged over the last year, as well as your joint work with members of this Committee, and many months of consultation with key stakeholders, to help advance issues of special concern to Native Americans.

I want to acknowledge and applaud in particular two of your most important legislative collaborations: S. 919, the subject of our legislative hearing today; and, S. 1352, the Native American Housing Assistance and Self-Determination Act, voted to be reported out favorably by this Committee several weeks ago. I am an original cosponsor and strong supporter of S. 919 and S.1352, major legislative priorities for tribal governments and native communities across the nation.

I look forward to hearing from the witnesses today. I will continue to work with you, other stakeholders and my colleagues to ensure that Congressional actions are guided by the principles of self-determination and self-governance, and the special political relationship between the United States and Native Americans remains strong.

Finally, as I may not have another opportunity to address you as Chair, I want to take this opportunity to formally thank you Senator Cantwell for your very able leadership of the Senate Committee on Indian Affairs; and, to acknowledge your proven commitment to American Indians, Alaska Natives and Native Hawaiians.

I look forward to working with you in the future to help build stronger and more self-sufficient native communities, create much needed jobs, and further strengthen our national economy.

Thank you.

––––––

PREPARED STATEMENT OF HON. TOM UDALL, U.S. SENATOR FROM NEW MEXICO

I would like to thank Chairwoman Cantwell for her leadership on S. 919, the Department of the Interior Tribal Self-Governance Act of 2013. I am proud to cosponsor this important legislation. Thank you Chairwoman Cantwell and Vice Chairman Barrasso for taking the time to hold a hearing on this legislation.

I am glad to see my friend Assistant Secretary for Indian Affairs, Kevin Washburn, here today. I understand that he will share a message of support from the administration. I would like to thank him and his team for working with tribes from across the country to reach agreement on the provisions in this bill.

Self-governance has proved to be a powerful asset to tribal nations. Since the enactment of the Indian Self-Determination and Education Assistance Act in 1975, tribes have shown the great accomplishments that can be made through self-governance.

Self-governance allows tribes to take control of the programs tribal members depend on, and to better direct the future of their communities. But beyond empowerment, self-governance has direct impact on tribal economies and employment.

As many have noted, A 2004 GAO report showed that tribes engaged in self-governance had greater gains in employment and per capita income levels from 1990 to 2000 compared with other tribes.

S. 919 seeks to improve self-governance contracting through the Department of the Interior. I believe this is an important step for tribes and the administration, and I am proud to be a cosponsor of the bill.

RESPONSE TO WRITTEN QUESTIONS SUBMITTED BY HON. JON TESTER TO
RONALD TRAHAN

Question 1. Chairman Trahan, there have been some recent setbacks in negotiations in the annual funding agreement between your tribe and Fish and Wildlife Service over the management of the Bison Range Complex. The work has been done, I think it was a positive step in the right direction. I would like to hear some more on the National Bison Range Complex and how Indian Country can work with the U.S. Government to increase access and appreciation for public lands, such as the National Bison Range.

Answer. Our FY 2009–11 Annual Funding Agreement (AFA) with the U.S. Fish & Wildlife Service (FWS) for the National Bison Range Complex (NBRC) was rescinded on procedural grounds by a federal district court decision in September 2010. The court did not find any problems with the AFA; instead, it found that FWS had not properly explained its invocation of a categorical exclusion under the National Environmental Policy Act (NEPA). After the court decision, FWS and CSKT negotiated a new agreement. Once we had negotiated a new draft AFA, we encouraged FWS to prepare an Environmental Assessment (EA) for the action in accordance with NEPA. The Tribal Council continues to fully support the preparation of an EA, but we have been frustrated by repeated delays in completing the process. Both FWS and CSKT have agreed that we had a very productive partnership at the NBRC while the last AFA was in place. It should therefore not take this long for us to return to that productive partnership. It is our hope that FWS will not announce any further delays and that this process will be completed this year.

In response to the second part of Senator Tester's question, I believe that, if federal agencies were more open to partnering with Indian tribes, the Tribal Self-Governance Act could be a great tool for augmenting federal resources for land management. Tribes can be effective allies in helping raise public awareness about public lands, including access to those lands. Tribes can add to public lands visitor experiences by helping to educate people about the lands' traditional cultural history, uses and importance. In short, CSKT believes that, in certain cases, Tribal Self-Governance affords federal agencies unrealized opportunities to further improve public lands management.

Question 2. In your testimony you talked about, and this is for you again, Chairman Trahan, you met with the Fish and Wildlife Service recently, maybe even today. And you continue to work on negotiating the annual funding agreement. I think everybody on this committee wants to see that through, I know you guys want to see it through. Could CSKT be able to provide the Committee with a progress report in early summer, where things stand on the Bison Range agreement?

Answer. Sure. We would be happy to do that in the early spring to late summer.

We expect that a briefing would be in order sometime this spring. Since the hearing, we have contacted the U.S. Fish & Wildlife Service and officials from its Denver Regional Office have indicated they would be happy to provide a joint update at that time.

Question 3. The Salish Kootenai tribes have some experience the Mission Valley Power. As we talked about earlier, I think the work you have done there is pretty impressive. I think it provides a model of how Indian Country can really work with State and local governments and do it in a way that I think helps everybody. Could you tell a little bit more about how operating this public utility has affected the tribe's relationship with the surrounding community?

Answer. We could do that in writing, but I could give you a short version. It has made a lot of difference within the community, because it has brought the communities more, they understand that the tribe is not trying there to hurt them, it is trying to be helpful to everyone. That is what it has done, it has kept the rates low and everything else in that perspective.

So it has kind of got rid of the big scare that everybody thought there was there with tribes managing something like that.

Question 3a. And just out of curiosity, how much of that power is used on tribal lands and how much is used off of tribal lands? Do you know that off the top of your head?

Answer. Mission Valley Power (MVP) is a federally-owned electrical utility celebrating its 25th year under Tribally-contracted management. CSKT contracts MVP operations from the Bureau of Indian Affairs under Title I of the Indian Self-Determination and Education Assistance Act (ISDEAA)?. MVP provides electrical power to almost the entire Flathead Indian Reservation, which has a population of 28,359 according to the 2010 census. MVP employs around 80 people, with total revenue of $25,876,105 in FY 2012. It should be noted that CSKT does not keep any of that revenue as profit—the money stays within the federal program. MVP does not keep track of the Indian or non-Indian status of its customers, but it currently services 19,400 electrical meters, serving over 16,500 customers. CSKT Tribal membership is currently around 7900 people, with roughly half of that 7900 living on the Reservation. Consequently, and as stated at the hearing, even when taking into account the Reservation residents who are members of Indian tribes other than CSKT, MVP has more non-Indian customers than Indian customers.